Love of Finished Years

Love of Finished Years

Messages between Soul Mates

Diane De Pisa

RESOURCE *Publications* • Eugene, Oregon

LOVE OF FINISHED YEARS
Messages between Soul Mates

Resource Publications
An Imprint of Wipf and Stock Publishers
199 W. 8th Ave., Suite 3
Eugene, OR 97401

www.wipfandstock.com

PAPERBACK ISBN: 978-1-6667-3035-7
HARDCOVER ISBN: 978-1-6667-2175-1
EBOOK ISBN: 978-1-6667-2176-8

NOVEMBER 1, 2021

A version of the following poems was published or recognized as indicated:
"One at a Time," "Winnowing," and "Life is But a Dream." *The Neovictorian/Cochlea* Vol. VII no.1, Spring-Summer 2003.
"Lapping Lethe." *The Neovictorian/Cochlea* Vol.VII no.2, Spring 2005.
"In Search of Time Past." *The Neovictorian/Cochlea* Vol. IX no. 1, Fall-Winter 2005-2006.
"Cypresses of Provence." *Little Red Tree International Poetry Prize Anthology* 2010.
"Home Thoughts from Hawai'i." *Little Red Tree International Poetry Prize Anthology* 2012.
"Bird Tracks: A *Pantoum*" won Poetry Society of America's Louis Hammer Award for a surreal poem in 2010.

"Come to me in the silence of the night;

Come in the speaking silence of a dream;

Come with soft rounded cheeks and eyes as bright

As sunlight on a stream;

Come back in tears,

O memory, hope, love of finished years."

FROM "ECHO" BY CHRISTINA ROSSETTI

Contents

Acknowledgments

MANY THANKS TO FRIENDS who read my manuscript and offered their encouragement and critiques. These include my Berkeley writing workshop colleagues Sue Austin, Susan Nunes, Joan Mastronarde, Mary Parks, Kaye Sharon, Dorty Nowak, and Mary Heller; my former pastor, Ron Sebring, who assured me that this work would be of value to others; Jocelyn Waller, hospice chaplain and bereavement counselor, who comforted me and encouraged my writing; Kris Dickinson and Nick Cedar, photographers who knew and loved my late husband and helped me in numerous ways. I am grateful to you all for convincing me that my personal saga might be of interest to others—and helping me find the phrasing and layout to best communicate it. You are teaching me indeed that no one is an island.

Acknowledgments

Introduction

Open Heart

One at a Time

What compels me to write
so often to you
since you died?
Perhaps like Sartre I try
to save myself
from undertows that drown:
flashes of your impish smile
and sudden laugh,
your last gaze grazing mine.

I follow your example
of being one-pointed,
tackle a feeling at a time,
skewer each emerging emotion
with a couple of lines—
like the Inuit with a spear
intent on one hole in the ice
where the seal comes up
to breathe.

I HAD A FORETASTE of widowhood in 1997, when Elio underwent heart surgery. We had dismissed his symptoms as signs of bronchitis and pinned our hopes on abstention from smoking and adherence to wine-drinking—the latter a favorite home remedy in his native Rome, following the adage that *il vino fa buon sangue:* wine makes good blood. We felt confident about the angiogram, performed on a Friday. When the doctors showed us a diagram of multiple artery blockages and set an appointment to operate on Monday, Elio remained calm but I felt stunned and suddenly dizzy. Three friends had lost their husbands in the previous three years. I wondered how they could survive such a blow, but realized vaguely it might hit me some day. In the future. Another day.

Now, after the brief weekend, Elio's demise loomed imminent. Maybe it would come this very day that was dawning grayly over the Golden Gate Bridge as I drove to the hospital. When I noticed the Kaiser HMO emblematic sunburst, I remembered that Elio's name came from Helios, the Greek sun god. Then the clouds split and the city was strafed with hopeful rays.

Throughout that endless Monday I wielded the two-edged sword of imagining life without my husband. As an impromptu ploy for self- preservation, I envisioned a future: the purge of his collections and trips to places he would not visit. I also conjured the deafening silence, the unspeakable sadness of his abandoned belongings. Then my focus telescoped to his body on the operating table. Was our thirty-nine-year saga about to end: our shared love of nature and animals, our laughter and trivial fights, our search for spiritual growth? His life, so markedly unique—confident, compassionate, irascible, and irritating—was caught in the impersonal gears of fate, one of billions bouncing in the universal hopper. With a flick he could be jettisoned. A presence that I had assumed to be permanent now revealed itself utterly frail and transient. I could foresee the numbing aloneness. Then I felt a superstitious guilt. By imagining his death might I not be conjuring it? I meditated for hours and gradually the niggling thoughts simmered down.

In the intensive care unit, before Elio regained consciousness, I held his hand and babbled assurances in Italian: "*Stai bene. Ce l'hai fatta.*—You're okay. You made it!" His chest was heaving, thanks to the labors of a respirator. The hand I held was cold because his temperature had been reduced for the surgery. Back in the waiting room a family was sobbing. The pall of death did not lift until Elio came to, complaining that breathing was a chore now that he was off the machine. He said he'd felt bad to leave me alone but added, "I wasn't scared. They couldn't do in the real Me."

We had undergone a crisis and shared a close moment. But within a month we resumed old habits: the bickering, the TV, the Italian preoccupation with food. Again we took life together for granted with its many little intimacies, such as my delivery of his morning juice in bed. I used my dry run into widowhood as material for a novel I was writing.

~

In 2002 the real death experience hit. As in 1997 I felt the vertigo, sought signs and transcendence. But there was much more. As before, Elio's symptoms were ambiguous. He had an allergic reaction to a medication, then a minor stroke, which compromised use of his right side. On April 1 the source was traced to a brain tumor. In hospital Elio contracted a staph infection but it was masked by anti-inflammatory drugs and he came home. He regained the use of his right hand and was optimistic. However, a biopsy revealed cancer in his lung, and we wondered why he grew weaker as we went regularly for his brain radiation treatments. On April 30 an ambulance took him back to the hospital. The staph was discovered, but now his immune system was too weakened to fight off the spreading cancer. Elio died on May 14. In a few weeks he had gone from recovering stroke patient to a corpse, toppled by a domino series of unsuspected ills.

As his life guttered, his body enmeshed with tubing, Elio's spirit was not dragged down. He greeted hospital staff cheerfully, praised adept nurses, inquired often of his doctor, "How are you?" Once or twice he asked, "What's the next step? " Then he'd remember, as if he'd mislaid a bit of minor information: "Oh, yes, I'm dying. " His courage and patience aroused my admiration, even as I felt cold fear at the prospect of losing him. When anyone expressed care beyond the call of expectation, Elio wept. Some saw this as a sign of weakness and urged him to be strong. I knew instead that his heart was opening in a new way.

Among the attendants was a young man from Kenya named Victor, who was especially gentle when he bathed Elio or changed the sheets. Even in his agony, Elio was able to appreciate this attention. He said, "You're a great man." Later I concluded a poem to Elio: "These words made you a victor too."

I slept on a chair in the hospital room and asked friends to relieve me for an hour or so each day. He did not want to lose contact. Once when I returned from a break he scolded, "I might have died!" Perhaps I was hoping he would slip away when I wasn't looking—a typical exit according to some nurses. But on May 14 Elio waited until I got back from my break. He opened his eyes once and I said, "Hi." It should have been good-bye; just then he drew in and gave up his last breath.

Most widows I know felt stunned for a year or more after losing their husbands. Several became reclusive. I, instead, seemed to have awakened from a slumber. Complacency was sloughed off during Elio's terminal weeks. I felt fear and disorientation but there was no temptation to be sedated or escape from thinking about Elio's life and death. I was catapulted into a sort of emergency mode and an acute awareness of my own mortality. Since Elio had crossed a boundary, I strained to know what was on the other side. If I stayed alert, the occult might reveal itself, rare as a comet flashing across the horizon.

The years since Elio's death have been filled with many vivid dreams and apparent signs from him. The first serendipitous discovery was that of a huge envelope addressed "To Elio from Elio." It was among cards I had saved over some twenty years, yet I had never seen it. Inside was the image of a Phoenix, the mythological bird that rises from its own ashes and flies to the city of Heliopolis in Egypt. Elio had written a "reminder" to himself that "after the fire has consumed the gross matter that creates flames . . . only the

Self shall be." I shared his message with the friends who gathered to honor his memory.

Many widows feel anger toward their husbands for leaving them. I never did, nor do I suffer survivor guilt. His death, however, released a horde of feelings, including anger for his past transgressions and regret for mine. Tears, which I had not indulged in for years, came down in monsoon proportions. I was obsessed with reviewing the forty-four years we spent together: I perused old photos, heard tape recordings, read cards and letters. I tried to judge whether ours had been a successful and happy marriage. The verdict fluctuated wildly. It still does. And so do my moods, along with the memory of him: a sunny, compassionate man who could yet be hyper-critical and overbearing.

There does not seem to be a sequence to grief. Various aspects cycle in orbit: nostalgia, anger, loneliness, regret, and transcendence. Writing offers a way to examine, sift, and cook raw experience, making it more digestible, if not palatable. At times I give vent to raw emotion, at others I wax philosophical. I have written over three hundred poems to Elio and continue to address him in my journals. Re-reading all this, I see that some of it has to do with the breakdown of bereavement, some with a build-up of recovery. There are so many feelings, often ambiguous or conflicting, that I crave order. So, to untangle the confusing strands of grief, I have organized excerpts from poems and journal entries into six chapters: three on themes of breakdown and three on build-up. Although I have juggled sequence and inserted poems into prose passages, I have kept the original direct address. Some of these are responses to his apparent communications to me. Hence the sub-title "Messages between Soul Mates."

After the training required to earn a PhD from UC Berkeley, I am inclined to be skeptical about what cannot be documented. Nonetheless, I have experienced many extraordinary coincidences, which I call Signs—most more blatant than the Phoenix card—and a hundred or so extraordinary Dreams. Many of these are uncannily vivid, unlike any I've had before. In most I am convinced I am awake and Elio has miraculously survived. When I do awake,

I have to recall details such as his cremation to establish that in "reality" he is dead.

The world we know is relative to our state of consciousness. I am grateful that in later life, after being educated to perceive a narrow spectrum of reality, I am being nudged to know wider possibilities, even if through a fearful journey. I cannot posit a theory as to how I remain in touch with Elio, but believe that something other than wishful thinking is involved. Signs usually occur when I'm not looking for them. The most vivid Dreams crop up spontaneously between sleeping and waking.

Most widows whom I know have had some such indication of their husbands' survival. Not many admit it publicly. I wish that by sharing my brushes with mystery I may encourage others to take heart from theirs. I hope, too, that by sharing my regrets and anger I may come to terms with them and foster equanimity also in others who have been bereaved or are about to be.

Communications between Elio and me are personal, but the time has come to share them with everyone who cares to be included. I don't pretend to offer advice for overcoming grief. I have not gone beyond my own. However, there have been breakthroughs, not so much to acceptance as to awe before the mystery of mortality. I have come to embrace, not death specifically, but the human condition, which includes it. I want especially to remind the bereaved that pain is an opportunity for growth and that what is lost can be found.

∽

Love of Finished Years

Messages between Soul Mates

Chapter 1
Vertigo

Incubus

To say *death*—yours—
mortifies me,
makes me want to faint.
It sucks the breath
from my body
and draws the mind
to a nether world.
It freezes my heart,
arouses attachment
to morbidity.
It seduces memory,
makes it forget
the joy of living.
Like a jealous lover
it dominates, this word,
until I keep company
only with it.

WHEN YOU WERE DYING the whole world began to change, to lose its safe, familiar face. It became cold and alien; I felt disoriented in the supermarket, at work, in the garden. As I noticed this strangeness creeping in I wrote **Something New**. After you died, I put the bottom line into the past tense:

There's a shiver among the leaves,
a bitterness in the breeze,
an austerity in the great tree
that was not there before.
A well loved soul
has passed from the world.

Shortly after you died, I thought I might feel your presence on Old Quarry Trail because we had been on it recently together. Instead, your absence there was palpable. It was a hot day, the path between dry weeds rather steep, as you may remember. I paused in the shade to catch my breath, the way we used to do, and perused the shadows, vainly, for some hint of you. After a while I attained an overview with Mount Diablo in the depths. Suddenly it struck me: In all those hills and valleys—and in the whole world—no trace of you can be found. I gasped, light-headed.

On the day of the Big Sale, when I was finally to get rid of extraneous items you collected over the years, I woke up too dizzy to move. Some friends thought it was due to guilt for selling off your stuff. I recovered in time for the sale, though, and have not had any more episodes. Life goes on, as if normal. I even cope with technical problems—although I don't have fun with them as you did. Perhaps you are helping me; in one of our last conversations you said you would. I don't doubt my ability to survive financially or deal with the exigencies of everyday life. I do not need you. I need only that you *be*.

That, of course, is the source of the shock: your inexplicable inexistence. Death seems a kidnapper, a magician who shoved you back into his hat never to see daylight again. Like Orpheus, I rage blindly through an underworld, calling a name that echoes; only I do not have a lyre with which to tame the Furies. How could you just disappear and not come when I cry out? What you've done is uncharacteristic, outrageous: Death is not something you can retract. The freakish finality of it induced a fear that haunted me for months and still comes back in weak moments:

Fear that I've misplaced you
in vast, mysterious realms

while the thought to follow after
strikes terror and overwhelms.

I tried to reason that fear has to precede courage, which otherwise has no meaning, and wondered—since I was fulfilling the prerequisite—when courage would click in. Many cross-currents of anxiety buffet me. Sometimes I think I'll drown in them:

On the ocean of grief
swells of sorrow
strike broadside,
memories swamp,
sobs dance like dinghies
on choppy seas.
I sink beyond my depth.

In the middle of cooking or weeding, I'll mutter a rune: "You won't be coming home; you're gone." Of course I don't need a reminder. I am testing my strength as I might after being bedridden, checking to see when these words will stop knocking the wind out of me—but they still do. Occasionally I lie in bed late and feel the waves of pain press behind my eyes and rock my heart. But then an impetus to move arises, I get up, and perhaps write you a poem or even make the bed. Writing about my feelings takes the edge off them. Wallowing in pain immobilizes, but acknowledging it energizes:

I have been kicked out of complacency,
booted from banality.
I rebound from inertia
with the stinging spring of pain.

What should I call this poem? You always gave succinct titles to your hermetic verses. Do you think **Swift Kick** would do the trick? I'm trying to say there's a sort of tough love working through your death and my suffering, forcing me to wake up and smell reality, which includes mortality.

I catch myself rationalizing that I am lucky to live where women are not buried or burned with their husbands. But I soon get fed up with such pep talks and continue to bump against the blunt fact that you are gone and some day I will go. The enormity of it intrudes especially between sleeping and waking, when I'm helpless:

> They come at dawn
> before I get my thinking cap on,
> children stealing into mother's bed:
> Brother Fear and Sister Sorrow.
> They crowd my space,
> press against my heart.
> I wake with the pulse of dread
> as if intruders prowled the house.
> Then I recognize these twins of mine
> and go back to sleep again.

Waking up and realizing you're not here is a shock I go through each day. I feel like a baby cast up from the amniotic sea, bewailing separation:

> Just so I am birthed each day
> from amorphous nights of dreams
> where you are still afloat,
> to face the dawn of exile.

After I finish teaching a class I walk out, fast as usual, but then recall that you're not waiting for me at home. Suddenly my verve slackens. I lose momentum, as if a dragline has attached itself to my heels. It's strange how an absence feels heavy. Snubbed up to the immovable fact that you are gone, I strain to deny myself denial, yet can't deny that I crave contact. I feel a morbid compulsion to review the last glimpses of you and all the stages leading to your diagnosis. Do you know it was on April 1 that cancer was discovered on the brain scan? You took the radiation bravely, called it a miracle when you could write again, were even optimistic when the oncologist said you had a thirty percent chance of recovery. And I was naively hopeful too, mesmerized by wishful thinking. April Fools!

It took a while to drum up the courage to look at those final photos that I snapped of you a few weeks before your death. You are obviously weak and seem to stare at the camera with "good-bye" written all over your face. Other images of the last days crop up repeatedly—for example, the morning when I woke up early to see your forehead pale as a skull and realized you were dying.

Films and poems about death take me back to your bedside. In one Italian movie, parents gather around their son's coffin and peer down at the body. I realized

one thing I could not do
was gaze upon you afterward;
kiss your pale, unfeeling brow;
stroke your numb, cooling hand.
I could not look in the face
you used to wear
knowing you were not there.

Even after I had disposed of your ashes, I would stare in amazement at photos, not reconciled to the destruction of your body: smooth, youthful lips; rascally wisps eluding your hat; the forget-me-not blue of your eyes, which could turn to ice in anger or melt in amusement.

They melted indeed
the day your body was burned—
fragile jellies in the furnace.
Even your trunk charred,
shuddered, collapsed.

The bag of ashes they gave me
bore no resemblance
to the you I knew,
sweet as a sun-kissed fig.
Can I be blamed if
I return again and again
to pluck forbidden fruit
from the fire?

I don't brood all the time, miss work, or avoid outings with friends. But in the background there is always the nightmarish awareness that something vital is missing—and the effects of that lack are cumulative. As the years roll by, I continue to question the long-term effect of grieving:

> Can it be the weight
> of years to come
> or memories
> that crowd my chest?
>
> Maybe it's the thousand days
> since you died
> that gather like snow
> to crush a roof.

Perhaps you will think it is unhealthy to focus on oppressive feelings. You never indulged in regrets or wishful thinking. Ceaseless mourning is unhealthy, but should I ignore my spurts of grief? If I try to hold them down I will always be walking on eggshells. When you died I felt off balance, as if I were teetering on a cliff. I can see how fear of the void can make a person turn to negation or rage. I choose to peer over the cliff. Fear has some perks—like that "spring of pain" that propels me out of old routines. Confidence grows as I continue to survive grief. Alternation of sorrow with meditative lulls reminds me of how samurai swords are made tough and flexible—like your homemade pasta! You may recall the documentary film we saw of the swords being heated, folded, hammered, and firmed in cold water.

> At times the hot tears flow
> even while serenity prevails,
> tropic rains
> coating cool windowpanes.
> These shifts
> from agitated heat
> to dousing cold
> temper endurance
> fold on fold.

So, dear Elio, at times I quail and at others derive strength by facing fear—but I can never forget that death is a mystery. Perhaps by lingering at the portals I will gain a glimpse of what lies beyond.

Chapter 2
Where Are You?

Stamped

I woke at dawn
and saw death's print
pale as ivory on your brow.

You lived a week or so
but you'd been claimed.
Nor friend nor I nor medicine
could put the color back
that death had mailed away.

Now I ask
where did death
send your glow,
your thoughtful frown,
the arpeggio
of your sudden laugh?

I KEEP ASKING MYSELF: Where did you go? I can see now why that
question is such a big theme in literature, as when Hamlet asks the
jester's skull: Whatever happened to your jokes? Remember how
we used to cry while we listened to Garcia Lorca's poem about a
murdered gypsy, especially the lines: *"viva moneda que nunca/se
volverà a repetir*—living coin that will never be minted again"? We

mourned that young man whom we'd never met because Lorca made him live for us. It's impossible to imagine that the vividly alive can suddenly disappear. I don't know if you ever saw my old poem about death. I called it *Sly Swiper* because death seems to be hoarding our treasures somewhere beyond our reach: dad's devotion, friends' humor, the dog's rambunctiousness. For Pepa pup I wrote, "The Bright One who flashed in you and shone/has cast your shape away/but somewhere dances on." But where *does* the Bright One dance, and how much of the familiar individual is there? I wish you could tell me outright.

While you were dying, on short breaks from the hospital I sat on our deck to soak in some sun. I felt despair because you were withdrawing from this bright world of flowers and butterflies. The weather was too fair, sunny from early morning on, and it seemed we should be planning a walk or a trip to the beach. The serene garden reminded me of a Japanese film (perhaps *Chushingura?*) in which noble men commit ritual suicide while pink petals fall from an azure sky. Such loveliness, from which they—and you—were wrenched!

I felt the wrench also on your behalf. I don't know if you were aware of the weather or even indulged in regret to be leaving the world. I do recall a final moment of enjoyment before the terminal trip to the hospital, when you looked through the window in the back door and saw the freesias suddenly sprung from bulbs. You had been pacing the house, regaining use of your right side, and were surprised by your favorite reds and yellows. You exclaimed, "*Che bei fiori!*" I wonder if you can still see flowers—or remember me, who planted the freesias. Now I sit on the deck and hope that somehow you may vicariously enjoy the garden, this *Locus Amoenus*:

> I sit in my circle of familiars:
> cats courting on the terrace,
> crows nesting in a big pine tree.
> To the south I see
> green of *bonsai* and ivy,
> in the east deep pink and white

of cosmos where they sway,
and north at my elbow there's
rosemary *for remembrance.*
The breeze brings news
of fragrant flowers
and children's mewls:
a little world entire—
if you were here.

While walking on the bayside trail that witnessed so many of
our wanderings, I can almost hear you ask me to pose for a picture
with green and gold fennels towering over me, exuding their lico-
rice odor. At home there are even more familiar rituals that make
me look toward the empty space where you always were. Meals,
that used to be a kind of communion, are secularized now. There
is no one with whom to break bread, share wine. Such meals seem
a sort of sacrilege, an Ex-communion. Another moment when I
feel your absence keenly is at sundown, on **Closing the Curtains:**

A gesture so simple yet defined,
to pull a cord
and close out
the coldness
beyond.

An action at each day's end
that marked the hour
when you and I
would settle in
together.

A ritual whose meaning is reversed,
to signify your absence
from this house,
my enclosure here
alone.

Once in a while in the little Chinese market up the street I
find a huge, juicy peach like the one I was eating when you first
came to pick me up at my *pensione*—how many years ago? I still

cherish how you appreciated my unselfconscious enjoyment. You said that Roman girls were more concerned with decorum, but you preferred my innocent sensuality. I wonder how I would have felt if I'd known then that we would marry and some day (today!) I would be mourning because

nothing remains of us
but memories
and so many reminders
like this enormous peach
that I hold in my hand.

I felt your absence keenly in 2005 when I visited Provence and saw again European **Red Poppies**, poignant reminders of our trips.

They blew in Majorca,
beckoned, bled,
spurted at our ankles
amid the grain.
They throbbed,
our passion pulsed.

In Ostia Antica
they marked our final year,
staining dry grasses
between the little
oven tombs.
Now in the harsh Var fields,
three years after
your body fell to ash,
they drench the dusty greens,
they dance en masse.
And still they bleed,
they bleed.

Nothing evokes loss more than the disposal of personal property. As I gave your favorite things to friends or packed apparel for charity, your character emanated from every item: your artistic bent in photos and jewelry you'd crafted, your love for the outdoors in hiking boots and sticks, your enjoyment of cooking in a shirt reserved for the kitchen. It seems strange that objects survive while their owners drop away, leaving only the trace of a hand on a sculpture, the imprint of a foot in a slipper, the modification in a piece of equipment. Handwriting is especially evocative. I keep running across old recipes, poems, letters—and I pause to ask: Where is the hand that wrote these?

I identify with the wind, invisibly frisking every leaf and grass blade, trying to track down that other dimension, the hiding place of the dead. Where did your habits and tastes go: your joy as Schubert's strains stride in and your smile of amusement when Me-u was on a rampage, "wound up" as you put it? I find it preposterous that, after some forty years of tuning in to your moods, now I don't even know if you are homesick. Like death itself you have become a mystery. I am at a loss even to imagine who, or what, or if you are. The old fear comes back, of having misplaced you somewhere off bounds to me.

Sometimes I try to configure what the afterlife may be like. If you are still around, why are you invisible? Are you made of some kind of energy unavailable to my senses? Is there an astral body? If the dead exist in some manner, I want to know what the experience is like for you. The ancients claimed the dead cross a river. I wonder if the other side resembles the meditative state.

Lapping Lethe

In the nether world
there's movement
as of light liquids
flimsy as mists
yet compelling
as any tide.
The mind, unmoored,
meanders adrift
blind to landmarks.
A thought like a log
floats by and then
is lost to view.
I wonder,

are these the waters
through which you wade,
memory of me
a fitful dream
in the midst of
subtle, compelling chaos?

I would like to know if there are breakthroughs for you as
there are for me when I have a vivid dream. Some gurus claim that
such encounters take place on the astral plane. When I inexplica-
bly have gooseflesh I think perhaps you are dreaming of me. Then
I imagine that when you re-awake in your dimension I fade like a
phantom, details of the dream dissolve in your light, and memory
melts in your day.

Oh, those details! It is a blessing to savor them in dream. But
I miss them at other times, so I gaze at photos and conjure memo-
ries. There is cat-man in love with Me-u, taking photos of her
many postures. There is the gardener, clipping thyme or rosemary
for a dish one of us is making. And there is the humorist, whose
laughter still echoes in the house.

Occasionally a witticism
crosses my mind
and I spit it out,
half expecting
to hear you chuckle.

I know your body's gone.
But laughter—
such a great survival tool—
how could it not survive?

We had our differences,
but one thing kept us
from coming unglued:
We knew how
to make each other laugh.

When I catch sight of your hats hanging by the door, I con-
figure your favorite pastimes and your last days. There's the ruby

beret, mate to my scarlet one, our signature headgear for winter walks. There's a brimmed canvas hat that ties on to resist the wind, fit to weather boat trips in Hawai'i and Italy. There's your favorite safari helmet, a sun filter that checkered your face with gold. And there's the cotton khaki cloche that you wore when wheeled to radiation treatments. It seems you went off absent-mindedly, leaving all your hats behind. What were you thinking?

Above all, photo albums evoke your uniqueness, reflecting changes as in slow motion cinema augmented by memories. In the earliest images you are young, slim, and tanned, playing matador with Rome traffic. Then you are leaping California creek rocks, gauging their slickness and your momentum. An endearing shot catches you prancing in place to Peruvian pipes. I envision you frequently in the kitchen, wearing an apron and kneading, stirring, tasting. A couple of pictures find you at table with glass raised toward me for a toast.

At a certain point the frames flicker fast forward. You are stuck in your seat, too weak to move, your normally robust arm trembling. Then I see the color fading from your face: a quick-fixed image before the unimaginable process of cremation. I wonder why any movie must end like that.

Nonetheless, I keep re-running the video to savor again your uniqueness, encompass your totality. Yet, even as I conjure the many images of you, I realize I am multiplying my griefs, mourning all the men you've been. I must admit

> I was wrong to screen your life in shards.
> It was a subtly mutating continuum,
> a filmstrip unwound to reach completion.
> Still I cut and edit stills
> to assuage my craving for re-runs.

On the other hand, snippets of memory assemble into an illusion of immortality. As I thumb through pictures of our wedding, thirty years' camping, and trips to Hawai'i and Europe, time is invalidated. The years are a flimsy fence, washed out by waters of remembrance.

15

But what if memory doesn't hold up? The prospect of plunging ahead alone is chilling. I remind myself,

look both ways.
It's a two-way street
leading back
to when we met
and forward
toward my death.
Your death is here—
a milestone,
perhaps half way
between my end
and our beginning
at sunny Roman bus stops.

When I think
of going on
year after year,
you in the rear-view mirror
dwindling,
I wonder:
how can I stop you
from falling off
the horizon?

Even if I do keep a hundred pictures clear in my mind, what is the value of a film loop playing *ad infinitum*? The dead can't deviate from old routines. And ultimately a kaleidoscope of memories does not reproduce that *viva moneda* because a person is more than a collection of traits. There is an elusive quality underlying all the quirks like the pervasive aroma of coffee, carrying more flavor than the sips. During your life, I took in your emanations, now distilled to core characteristics: tenderness, courage, and cordiality. This essential you imbued our daily rounds and lingers like a fragrance evoking your presence.

Sum of Parts

I miss you as I loved you,
not just for humor and kindness
nor in spite of anger and inconsistencies,
but for some unnamable essence
that made where you were home.
We were companions for life,
perhaps before and beyond it,
our names linked as proclamation
of a permanent partnership.
Two amounted to more than twice one,
your subtraction compounded
to more than that
of my other half.
Love and loss
defy reason and math,
assuming the air
of absolutes.

Rather than dwell on lack and loneliness, I prefer to assume you are here and can hear me, so I tell you what I've been doing or planning, whom I've seen, where I doubt, how I hope. I talk to you more than when you were alive!

Occasionally I catch myself in a phrase or intonation characteristic of you. I seem almost to be impersonating you when performing chores that you habitually did or photographing an angel trumpet. A couple of times I deliberately tried to channel you, lending you my flesh to allow speech, sight, even dance.

Déjà Vu

I made the mistake
of pretending I was you
soaking in the mellifluous notes
of your favorite flutes
and harps from Peru.
I closed my eyes and smiled
your little smile of rapture.

I merged with you in trance,
feinted, swayed and gyrated.
You were so much with me
that I shuddered
as one possessed
and was flooded
with tears.

Stymied in attempts to recapture you, I try to reconcile myself to the inevitability of your death. Especially after a bout of misgivings, when I think the doctors should have caught the staph infection earlier, I reason that no result has only one cause; fate may even have conspired to make the doctors drop the ball, insuring a quick death. I must accept the unforeseeable twists that unravel our lives.

Nonetheless, I am not reconciled to losing touch. I cannot say whether I expect to "see" you in a discarnate state or to encounter you in a future life. Sometimes I imagine the ideal *post mortem* encounter. I leap free of my body as from a sinking canoe and you grab my hand in yours, capable and quick as in life, and draw me into the rarefied ether where you have been waiting. Sometimes I urge you to come back; I make **A Plea for Reconstitution**:

If you have dissipated
like smoke diluted in ether
isn't there some way
you could collect yourself?

It seems not. You haven't appeared, except in my dreams.

Sages in all traditions say that time is an illusion: that from a superior perspective, past, present, and future co-exist. Sometimes I try to tap into this eternal present.

In Search of Time Past

What if the past
is no phantom
faded by time
but an entity

still in existence
as geologic layers
hidden from view?
There dreams on
our first encounter,
youth, union still intact,
and days in the sun-shot
tent by the river:
an underworld entire
waiting to be mined!

Then there is that other, less comforting view that we have
read and talked about: that we are dreamt into existence by a
divine entity or all-informing intelligence. So, I am hounded by
the question:

What happens, I wonder,
when that Great Mind
awakens, as it has in your case,
from the dream of our singular self?
For you now the answer
is either obvious or irrelevant.
For me—still dreamt but bereft
of the figment that was you—
to know is of the essence.

As you are aware, spiritual traditions have diverse takes on
the "awakening" from life's "dream." Some Buddhists claim we re-
incarnate after a month or two. Considering the Signs and Dreams
I still receive, this doesn't seem to be the case with you. It would
be bizarre to recognize you as a baby! Still I read all manner of
afterlife literature, eager for clues to your whereabouts. The mysti-
cal branch of Judaism offers two possibilities: a sort of permanent
heaven, or—failing that—repeated incarnations.

Paradise

(Heb. *pardish*)

Cabalists claim two Edens exist—
one all-the-way union with God,
the other a half-way place
where we cultivate our garden
before return earthwards.
Did you enter that first Eden at last—
or should we look for you
among earth-wanderers,
bearing fruits from the lower orchard?

My chief comfort is this: Even though sages do not agree altogether on our loved ones' destination, none of them denies its existence. Skeptics may claim that death is a dead-end street, but the wisest and happiest of people not only believe in consciousness independent of the body but recount direct experience of it in mystical states. It is frustrating to think that you *know* what afterlife is, yet apparently can convey only hints of it through Signs and Dreams.

Chapter 3
Balancing Acts

Winnowing

Shall I cherish the nurturing kernel
and reject the chaff that chafes—
remember you generous and kind,
forget the meaner moments?
Must I dump your coarse hulls
and flail you to saintliness?

I lived with you entire
and will remember you so:
whole grain.

WHY DID YOU HAVE to die? Did you have a "good" peaceful death,
as it seemed? Could we have saved you with prayer or alternative
medicine? Was it a demon or guardian angel who caused you to
die so quickly? Were you a good person? Was I a devoted wife
or a spineless wimp? Did I yield to your demands from love, or
fear of disapproval? How come I miss even your negative traits?
Why am I lonely now when, before, time apart sometimes seemed
a vacation?

Many other futile but obsessive questions arise in the silence
of your absence. What if you had lived a bit longer, hung on by a
thread, only to fall off in the end? The clean death was preferable,

objectively thinking. You hadn't been very creative for some time; were you getting by with a few oases of pleasure in animals, humor, and food? It seemed sad that heart medication made you vulnerable to sunlight: you whose symbol was the sun, whose tan gleamed dark as saddle leather when I first met you. Perhaps your soul grew impatient and refused to face more travail. You used to be playful, but

> In time your tally of tricks trickled away.
> When the jester no longer stepped forth,
> death found the coast clear
> to step in.

Of course the question of *why* you died is complex and ultimately unanswerable. But what about the *how*? Friends who arrived shortly after your death remarked on how peaceful you looked. I, who witnessed your departure, sometimes wonder about your final attitude:

> I see the last exhalation
> inflate your cheeks
> as if you would regurgitate.
> Meanwhile your eyes converge
> on that mid-point in the brow
> where the divine
> is said to reside.
> Did you leave enlightened,
> or just fed up
> with relative existence?

Did you give back breath to the cosmos as generously as you bequeathed your things? Were you reconciled to your fate, or merely resigned? You were always one to rally in necessity, to persevere, stay the course; as you would say, "*Quando stai in ballo, balli.*" If anyone could get his act together at the eleventh hour it would be you. But how could you cope with the unknown? You read some primers, principally *The Tibetan Book of the Dead*. Still, you wondered what awaited you: "*Chissà come sarà?*" I reminded you of what author John Neihardt told me as he approached death: "It will be a great adventure!" You did not quarrel with this appraisal, but you were not one to risk the untried if it could be avoided.

Wearied with afterlife prognoses, I often turn my gaze backward, to scrutinize the past—and judge our marriage. Was it a happy one or not? Often I felt frustrated. Instead of answering to my complaints, you took the offensive, pointing the finger at me. On the other hand, I must admit circumstantial evidence of how we enriched each other's life. I look around the living room and see our art work and mementos of our trips. Also, I rejoiced in your enjoyment (of certain things) more than in my own:

> There are reasonable doubts,
> making for a hung jury.
> Perhaps it's best to give up
> on reaching a verdict.

The fact is I do not give up. I seem fixated on arriving at a decision and re-open the case repeatedly. I deplore how I encouraged some of your bad habits and how you dragged me down to dull dates with the TV. I also count the ways in which we supported each other. It seems that I can't let go of forty-four years without accounting for them. We invested our vital force both in the better and the worse, and we both left important things unsaid and undone. I am bewildered at how much unexamined life still keeps coming to light:

> I supposed I would not suppress
> such a thing as a fractured self.
> But I did
> until you died
> and blew the lid
> off everything.
> The dense pellet
> that immured me
> in tearless oblivion
> exploded,
> revealing irrevocably
> sharp bits of anger
> and jagged jealousy
> embedded like old shrapnel.

I mourn not only the loss of you but lost bits of myself that got mangled in our marriage—and of course I tend to blame you. I marvel that a dead man can still break my heart! The upheaval caused by your death brings to the surface both happy and sad memories fossilized like shells in a midden, to be dug up and sifted. I hope that by examining our life together I can piece together its proper form. Perhaps my better self will emerge like gold undefiled by doubts.

I ask myself why I still dwell on satisfactions denied and other causes for bitterness. I never ceased to look forward to time spent in your company, although you disappointed me often. I am amazed at

> the perennial hope,
> like an unquenchable pilot light,
> that love harbors at its heart.

I try to laugh about how we annoyed each other, you calling me "*gatta morta*," your Italian version of *sly boots*, and I telling you how it's "in spite of everything" that I love you. There's no doubt that your death stirred things up. It feels as if a dam has burst and a wall of negativity and indifference has come

> tumbling down
> dissolved by the deluge
> of my tears.
> The breaking torrent
> bears fragments of us
> dating back to courtship days:
> endearments, imprecations—
> kaleidoscopic debris
> of all our years.

Borne by the impulse of grief, fresh feeling overwhelms me. Is it love? I think it may be. Nonetheless I continue to see-saw. The jury is still out on our marriage. One day I review photo albums and declare

This marriage has reached completion,
coming to term but not perfection—
an entity marred beyond recognition
at crucial points by inattention.

Another day I sit to meditate and say aloud, "*Ti amo*," then mouth
the "Me too" I always heard in reply:

We repeated it daily,
a reminder that we were
in the right place at the right time.
I have no idea where my words end up
but feel compelled to send them:
"*Ti amo*," it seems, forever,
even if "*anch'io*"
never echoes.

The marriage, like a partially solved jigsaw puzzle, is seamless
in some respects, yet loose pieces lie strewn about. You'd think that
in forty-four years there would have been time to resolve every-
thing, but this is not so:

It gives me pain
to lose the loving heart of you
and all inconsequential joys
of being two.

But more I dread the pang
of slur and slight
recalled in bitterness too late
to ever be put right.

The spilled milk syndrome floods also into recollections of
our on-off romance and how we are finally **Out of Touch:**

The scars that marred
 the surface of our world
diminish in perspective:
old bickering a dumb-show
glimpsed through cloud curtains;
years of being close, far, close
a minuet seen

through the wrong end
of an astronaut's telescope.
I'm falling in love once more
and yearn to be near you.
But I am an exile
and can never set foot again
on that planet where we
held hands and sparred.

And so it goes on: good marriage, bad marriage alternating
like the maiden and the witch on quaint barometers. When the
witch prevails, my criticism tends to digress from the marriage to
direct attacks on you. Why did you try to condition me to be cau-
tious and circumspect, although you claimed to have first fallen in
love with my unconformity? I suffocate on suppressed passions,
like strands of muscle snuffed out by **Heart Attacks:**

fibers numbed by old slights ignored,
bits that died bit by bit,
buried but unmourned.

Sometimes, when I miss you too much and find myself murmur-
ing endearments, I deliberately recall something venomous you
said. However, poison as an antidote to loss doesn't work very well.

Not that I'm prepared to let you off the hook altogether. I
just need to establish a balanced view. But you were an entity of
extremes. On the one hand there was the innocent in love with
his cat, who onomatopoeically said "cute"; and on the other, the
judge who sentenced my suggestions without trial. I grieve over
both members of this **Odd Couple:**

Why do I mourn Mr. Always Right?
Because, although so unlike you,
he disappeared in your company
and we never let him know
he was unworthy of you.

I have to conclude that you were a package of paradoxes—as
perhaps we all are. Although not always sensitive to my feelings,
you were always concerned for my welfare and reminded me to

drive safely as I went to work, promising me hot homemade soup when I came back. How it warmed my heart to have you wait up and know I was your all as you were mine!

Friends called you the Renaissance Man because of your many talents as pianist, sculptor, photographer, jeweler, and inventor. At your job in the *caffè* you dispensed solace and wisdom along with *cappuccini*. Several proclaimed you were an "old soul" who had been incarnated often. I could imagine you as Leonardo, that genius notorious for abandoning projects once he solved the salient problems. You did the same thing, and never profited professionally from many of your skills. You seemed reluctant to be confined to one role. If you were the reincarnation of several geniuses, you managed to replay your many motifs.

I am grateful to have shared my life with such a resourceful and creative person, although when you were here I didn't always appreciate you. Your death was a catalyst that reconfigured my psyche, ousting complacency and admitting compassion.

Extreme Unction

Your death,
shaking me from the roots,
has dislodged smallness,
hardness, and bitterness.
I break,
like olives beneath the wheel,
as you did at the end,
and shed tears
like precious oil
pressed from the heart.

On our last trip to Kauai, at the Hindu temple we were invited to put a petition on the altar. I don't know if you wrote one, but I begged, "Let me learn love," meaning not affection or infatuation, but a more profound acceptance of others. I forgot about this prayer and was soon preoccupied with the events leading to your death. Now I realize that my "sacrifice" has borne fruit: My obdurate heart has burst—I feel new stirrings of sympathy for women's weaknesses and old folks' insecurities—and you are the price I've paid for this bounty. So in a way my grief is graced with gratitude.

In the end I wonder why I persist in drawing up a balance sheet of praise and blame. After assessing your death and our life together, I realize the inadequacy of the intellect to deal with feelings. The important questions cannot be resolved, the pain assuaged, by tallying blessings and curses. Emotions run too deep. Healing starts on another plane—with Signs, Dreams, and Ceremonies.

Chapter 4
Signs

Bird Tracks

(excerpt)

Then ravens alit on the giant pine
next door, where Fran my friend declined.
They were too clearly a fatal sign
for her and for one more yet to find.

Next door, where Fran my friend declined,
they conferred darkly on a limb
for her and for one more yet to find
and fling beyond the world's bright rim.

I SELDOM THOUGHT OF portents before your death. Looking back,
though, I detect forewarnings beginning a year earlier when we
went to Italy:

> the dying kitten in Rome,
> the coffin lowered
> into the alley at Levanto,
> the yearned-for return
> home to learn
> your closest brother-friend
> had met his end.
> Then there were those

discarded cars on Kauai
half-covered in creepers.

I don't know why I didn't hear an alarm go off when you developed a tumor in your bladder. Perhaps you sensed a danger lurking there, but I was just glad the surgeon claimed to have removed it all and gave us the go-ahead for our trip to Kauai. It did strike me as strange that, although his news was supposedly good, he laid a sympathetic hand on my shoulder and said he'd be available if I needed to talk. He must have known that cancer travels around and surmised we'd be tracking it down eventually in brain and lung. His kind gesture comes back occasionally to haunt me—one of several subtle warnings that the end was just over the horizon.

Do you remember the picture on Lynda's last Christmas card—an Italian terrace with an empty chair? You were taken aback by this "*presagio infausto*," but of course our friend had not intended to send an ill omen and had no inkling that your chair would be vacant in five months.

The statuettes of Ganesha that you bought in Kauai that winter now seem to have hidden meaning too. You may remember the imposing black carving of the elephant-headed god seated amid flower offerings at the entrance to the Kauai Hindu ashram. The four-armed heavy-set deity lacks a tusk: a sacrifice. After our tour of that paradisal place, you sought out an image in the gift shop; later you bought another in a store. I put them both on the mantel: the brass one from the temple, seated and wearing a lei; and the other, an irresistible dancing Ganesha:

> Did you pick this particular patron
> through some intuition
> of your declining condition—
> Ganesha, Lord of Obstacles,
> who both poses and
> roots out opposition?

Shortly after we got back from Hawai'i I noticed two ravens in the big pine next door. We had just heard that Jocelyn's mother was dying. I thought: One raven has come for her but the second for someone else. I hope not Me-u. I'd not thought about Signs since your heart surgery five years before, but the ravens struck me immediately as premonitory. It was an ironical twist of fate that you, who wept when our aged friend chose hospice, died a month before she did.

Another uncanny Sign came a month after the ravens' visit, when you dropped a bottle of wine.

Launch

So unlike you
to lose your grip!
We didn't know
a stroke had hit
you broadside.
The bottle of Rioja
crashed from your hand
to christen the kitchen
with crimson streaks—
ill-starred send-off
on the sixty days
that sculled away
your life.

Of course there is nothing strange about a compromised limb fumbling an object. I don't know why, since your ills hadn't been diagnosed yet, I was seized by dread at the sight of those blood-red splatters sprayed all over cupboard doors, stove, refrigerator, and floor.

In retrospect it seems we had warnings but carried on with our habits as if nothing was wrong. And after you were diagnosed with cancer, we didn't put up a fight. Did we unconsciously accept what destiny mapped out?

There were some peculiarities about the last physician who treated you and eventually declared you dead. He didn't look like the other doctors but was stocky and young, like a wrestler—fit bouncer to usher one out of this world. When I heard his name—Dr.

Sarafian—I thought immediately of the seraphim. I remembered vaguely that these were the highest angels and that it was a seraph who laid a live coal on Isaiah's mouth and declared, "Lo . . . thine iniquity is taken away." I wrote of **Dr. Sarafian,**

He made no bones about the prognosis,
advised against life-prolonging ploys.
He dropped the bad news
like a hot coal
from the altar of God.
You were purged of trivialities,
put your mind to bequeathing
and concern for me.
True to his name,
the doctor proved to be
a messenger
of the highest order.

It is said that the seraphim have multiple wings. I remember how, many years ago, Reverend Becker, that famous psychic, told you that a spirit mentor was fanning you.

Phoenix, ravens, angel: Winged beings seem suited to conduct us from this life to the next. I wasn't looking for any more after you died. But then a hawk appeared about the time your body was cremated. I had seen perhaps one of these raptors above our yard in more than twenty years, but that day something induced me to look up. Against the rainbow haze around the sun there appeared a red-tailed hawk, pale and ethereal. It occurred to me it might be a Sign but I was not convinced until other hawks showed up when I was thinking of you.

Once, when walking with Jocelyn and Peter in a park, I saw three hawks and wondered: Where is the fourth? Shortly it came, gibbering, and circled above us as if intentionally bidding for attention. I began asking you to send hawks. In fact, while sitting on our deck in the early days, often I heard a distant shriek and saw a speck approaching from the direction of Albany Hill. Then this braying mote would wheel in close and I'd recognize a raptor announcing its arrival with shrill cries.

Birds figured also in the episode at our "summer home," the spacious campground by Stuart Fork. Our friend Theresa appealed repeatedly for a return to the Trinity Alps. Finally I gave in. It was now eight years since you and I had hiked there for the last time, and twenty since she had joined us. Theresa and I didn't feel up to a long hike so we were transported by horses to Salt Creek, where the packer left us and our stuff. Then we plowed down cross-country from the main trail, as we used to do, to reach the secluded campground by the river.

Soon we saw the enormous boulder that shadows the deep pool where we used to swim and you fished. Theresa said, "Do you think he'll send us a Sign?"

I had been wrapped up in navigating the unmarked route and had not been thinking about you. But then I felt you were there. Just downstream of the big emerald pool were three mergansers: two females with glowing chestnut heads and a greenish-headed male. Their crests stuck out behind them like starched kerchiefs. It was the first time I'd spotted that large, colorful species of duck in the thirty-some years we'd hiked in the Trinities. Did you send them as a memento of the three of us?

I assumed at first that "bird tracks" were your preferred Signs. But my attention is grabbed also by occasional odd, out-of-place objects. And by sudden chills or electric buzzes—sort of scary and impossible to ignore. I suspect your influence also when technical problems crop up, then fix themselves. And when uncanny coincidences occur. I assure you that I have picked up on your attempts to communicate and am grateful. Some Signs were pretty obvious!

The first odd *objet trouvé* was that three-inch jade-green crackle-glazed figure of a cat seated like a yogi. It was a few months after you'd died. I drove your car to meet Rebecca at the movies and parked it in a public garage. When we came out, there was a statuette on the engine hood facing the driver's seat. At first I mistook the ears for horns but then I saw it was a **Meditating Buddha Cat**:

It was just the sort of thing
you'd have picked up in a thrift store

as totem for us cat-loving amateur yogis.
Perhaps, as my friend suggests,
you sent it from that great
Goodwill shop in the sky.
Just in case, I placed it on the mantel
seated in lotus position
by the unsigned cat card
you'd addressed to me.
It seems to say in its silent way
what you would have written:
Be calm, be well, seek high things—
and don't forget your animal self.

Another object that intrigued me was the tarnished coin that
showed up inexplicably on the black onyx pedestal of the little
silver bust you made in jewelry class.

Spare a Dime

Since you've gone,
I'm always looking for a Sign.
This burnt-looking apparent penny
did not appear to be an auspicious one.
Thinking it might be the "telegram"
that in a dream you said you'd send,
I polished it. Still it was too dim.
Being a beggar for a message,
I scrutinized it under magnification.
The thin disk said "One Dime."
I insisted and made out "Liberty"
"In God We Trust" and "E pluribus unum."
What a windfall!
I couldn't hope
for better news of you.

Three years after your death, when I'd given up expecting any
overt Signs, I was startled by the most suggestive of all odd objects.
You know how I hate to get stuck in group activities. Atypically,
I had agreed to coordinate a church bazaar. Of course bazaars,
along with thrift stores and garage sales, were your favorite

treasure-hunting grounds, but I was too busy supervising the sale to think of you until my eye fell on a small glass vase that had been painted, perhaps by a child, in rainbow colors. I said to myself, "Elio would probably buy that." No sooner had I sub-vocalized your name than I spotted another identical vase on which ELI was spelled out in red nail polish, punctuated by a big red dot that signified the price—and completed your name: ELIO. I bought both vases and have them, filled with flowers from our garden, flanking your photo in the dining room.

Sudden chills came mostly in the early days and came so often that I can't imagine they occurred by chance. I called them by their Italian name: *brividi*. They occurred almost always after I finished several hours of teaching, when my mind turned to you. Once the students were out of earshot, I would whisper, "*Torno a casa.*" Then I felt the hair on my arms lift. It seemed you were waiting in the wings for my mind to turn homeward and then you rushed in before something else captured my attention.

Similar but much rarer are shocks like an electric current investing my whole body. This experience occurs in dreams or between sleeping and waking. Twice I felt the bedclothes lift, and once some power seemed to spin me on my back like a break-dancer. Several times I rallied to demand, "Who are you?" There was never an answer—but I remember you said one time that if you died you'd twitch my sheets.

If the dead have lapsed into a vibratory mode of existence, it seems logical that you might make yourselves felt as electric currents. Or as interferences in electrical appliances. Shortly after you died I was bedeviled by the fizzling of two favorite reading lamps, which I reluctantly replaced. After learning how a woman got signals from her deceased mother through electrical phenomena, I gave the lamps a second chance. There was nothing wrong with them. By then I was onto your tricks, so I wasn't too nonplussed when other appliances went dead and revived under their own auspices: the new electric heater, the furnace thermostat, the juicer, a telephone, a cabinet light, my car radio, more lamps. . . . All right, already!

Most peculiar was the case of your constant companion, the old-fashioned Canon camera. A student was interested in buying it and came to try it out. Katie took two pictures and then the film-advance lever went limp. In vain I consulted the manual and Jocelyn, who uses the same type of camera. Nick and Kris, as pros, pronounced the final *post mortem* and suggested I sell it for parts. However, after Katie served *pro bono* as my teaching assistant, I decided to have the camera fixed and give it to her. I took it to a repair shop, where the technician checked it. It was working. No repairs were needed. The lever had been loose and now it engaged. Katie has been using the Canon without problems for several years.

Finally, there have been inexplicable coincidences that seem to be more than that. I remember the caper you pulled the day friends came for your little at-home send-off when **No One Sat in Your Seat:**

> Your memorial went without a hitch.
> There was much beauty there:
> azaleas, roses, Hawaiian ginger,
> a small gathering of friends—
> Christian, Muslim, and Jew
> and a few skeptics too.
> Seating was tight but one spot
> on the loveseat stayed empty.
> Without knowing, all steered clear
> of where you used to sit.
> Were you there, as it appears,
> drinking in music,
> fragrance of flowers,
> and tears?

Two years later, at the anniversary dinner, I was moved by a similar coincidence. I had arranged a chair for everyone around the table, but a last-minute cancellation freed the seat facing me. Did you invite yourself? I strongly suspect you were here on that other occasion, when Christina unexpectedly sobbed suddenly as she was about to sit down to dinner. I had to tell her she had been placed where you usually sat. Although she isn't particularly credulous, I think she is unusually sensitive.

Perhaps that is why you were able to buzz Christina with sudden shivers at the moment of your death. She knew you were in critical condition but had no way of knowing, while driving her car in Washington, at what moment you passed away in California. Nonetheless, she suddenly cried, "*Ciao, bello,*" burst into tears, and went home to play Mozart's *Requiem.* She took note of the time—1:11—and I confirmed that her attack of grief struck at the moment of your death.

I've become a bit obsessed with this number, although I never paid heed to numerology. It seems I often chance to check the time at 1:11—or maybe 11:01 or even 11:11. Flight numbers for my trips have had multiple ones. The classroom where I teach regularly is number 111. The racetrack barn where I feed feral cats is 111. The street address of two favorite entertainment venues is 1111. Re-reading what we wrote in Glenn's house journal in Kauai, I see that our first joint entry was on January 1, 2001: 01-01-01; and our last entry was on January 11, 2002: 01-11-02. Come to think of it, your birth date was 11-15-34. Did friend Nino set up a precedent by dying on 06-11-01?

While planning an anniversary dinner, I took out the Tarot cards. Following the simplistic instructions in the pack, I got some messages that seemed better than coincidental: To quote the printed interpretations, you were "immersed in memories," having just had "a journey by water," leaving behind "folly and intoxication," aiming for "ecstasy," filled with "hope and creative intelligence," and "surrounded by friends"—appropriate scenario for a forthcoming gathering in your honor! The last and most important card that I drew was the Eight of Wands. When I saw all those sticks pointing toward the ground, I thought there must be some bad news. Instead, the wands are to be interpreted as *Arrows of Love.*

Synchronicities crop up other places besides in the cards—for instance, in the drawer next to your seat, now mine. One day, for the first time I noticed a little phone message tape in the drawer. On a hunch, I dug the relevant telephone out of the garage and plugged it in. The message light flashed and I pressed the play button. It was you, saying you were out shopping and I could expect you home about 12:30. I glanced at the clock and saw that it was exactly 12:30 then. Shivers! I tried to re-play the tape to hear your voice, but was unable. The tape had conveyed its message.

A couple of other times it seemed you sent me tapes on request, the way you sent hawks. Once, at bedtime, when I was lamenting aloud how lonely I felt and appealing to you for a Sign, I heard something fall in the other room. It was a tape you'd made in 1959, while we were separated. I played it without rewinding and caught the segment where you forecast that soon we would be "*uniti per sempre.*" Then you sign off for the day with a loving good-night. I went to sleep with uplifted spirits, sensing that we were indeed united forever.

Another memorable coincidence occurred on November 15, the date of your and Kaiumars's birthday, the first one after your death. I had cried all day, but rallied for dinner with Kaiumars and his family, grateful to be included. We were in Crockett at a restaurant frequented by typical Americans in sweat shirts and baseball caps. Then I caught sight of *Roma* emblazoned in gold and red on a young man's jacket. Later I wished I'd approached him to know if he was from your hometown and why he was wearing its soccer colors in suburban USA. Then I thought: It's okay; he has delivered his message.

More recently, while I was hanging photos for an exhibit of your work at *Caffè Mediterraneum* and thinking of how you had frequented its spaces for so many years, I was approached by a young man holding a portfolio of his own photos taken at Barak Obama's presidential inauguration. I admired how he captured many joyous faces at this historical event, and noted how these faces resonated with your own choice of happy images from the sixties. Then the young photographer introduced himself. His surname is Romano, born in Rome.

I often wonder by what occult mechanism such coincidences crop up and how you manage to convey messages from your new whereabouts.

Distant Feeling

Telepathy—what else
could bring your vivid image to mind
and electric shivers to my flesh?
You embrace, admonish, dance
with me in tactile dreams
and send cryptic signs by day.
Your ashes lie in a box
snowed under sympathy cards,
but you are not there.
When I cry out, "Where are you? "
you seem to reply,
with a touch of sarcasm,
that, like my own eyes,
you are invisible to me
but just as near.

Chapter 5
Dreams

In These Dreams

your existence is undeniable—
not that you do something special
but that I'm so sure I'm awake
when you make your appearance.
I am surprised, delighted,
and say, "Ah, you're back!"
We embrace and you
are solid to the touch.

Then you dissolve
and I come to, alone,
the episodes dwindling
like mists in the wind.

I sit bewildered, but almost convinced
I've digressed into other dimensions
where perception is acute
beyond our fondest dreams
and you are there
waiting for me
to break through.

A MONTH OR SO after Pepa died I had a vivid dream of her, in which I knew there was a discrepancy: The dog, who had been lame at the end, was bounding with youthful vigor. Since you died I have had perhaps a hundred such dreams, where I know you are supposed to be dead but are so real that I am convinced I'm not asleep. I call these Wakeful Dreams. I have also had a few Lucid Dreams, where I know I am dreaming but am sure nonetheless the encounters are real. Except for the one episode with Pepa, I have had Wakeful and Lucid Dreams only since you died. And in these Dreams you are always healthy, sometimes in your twenties, as when I met you, and sometimes in your prime. About a week after you died I had a Wakeful Dream:

> Early this morning
> electric shivers thrilled my skin,
> intimation of your imminent
> ingress for the first time
> into my dreams.
> I went back to sleep
> and there you were.
> It seemed I made the mistake
> of writing you off too soon.
> Clearly you had survived
> terminal illness.

Figuring, in my sleep, that I must have imagined you were dead, I was glad I had not discarded your things. Seeing how young you looked, I asked the date and you playfully replied, "Nineteen-sixty-four." Then we became involved in consulting calendars, trying to figure out whether we'd gone back in time or if you had returned from the dead.

In one early death-defying Dream it seemed you were determined to convince me of your presence, cropping up on the street, at the kitchen sink, finally in bed. Feeling your firm flesh, I was at last convinced you lived. In fact, frequently, as in this dream, there is intimacy. However, there is seldom eroticism, although in a typical Wakeful Dream you are my **Bedfellow**:

> Clearly, you were real,
> lying in bed by my side.

I could see the folds of your eye
as you recited an archaic poem
about someone "freaking" somewhere.
We cracked up over that one.
You were hearty and fleshy
so I knew I'd been deluded
to think you were dead.
Delighted to find you alive,
I pulled you into my arms
and hugged you to death.

In such Dreams there is no doubt in my mind that I am awake and I corroborate the fact by scrutinizing details of your face or body:

We were sitting on a bench
under a radiant sky.
I peered at you intently
to take in how
vividly real you were.
You asked what I was staring at.
I almost blurted
I thought you were dead
but held my tongue.
It was enough
that you weren't,
and that we were
together.

One extremely graphic and prolonged Dream harks back to the times when you worked late at the *caffè* and came home smelling of coffee. I heard the door open with a key and knew it was you. I called and you came immediately to bed, leaning over and on me weightlessly. We talked for some time and finally I exclaimed, "You were dead! You were in my dreams but now you're really here. I didn't even fall asleep tonight!" You confirmed my impression. We hugged and I could feel your arms tight around me, see your cheek, clean-shaven as in the early sixties. I asked if you could hear me when I talked to you. Your reply was ambiguous and you murmured something indistinct, which turned out to be *"Vuoi essere maltrattata?"* I asked why I had to think about being mistreated. Your reply was one I could not have invented: *"Perchè ci invecchiamo e ci consumiamo*—Because we grow old and wear out." Shocked by this dire pronouncement, I opened my eyes suddenly. As usual after a Wakeful Dream I could scarcely believe I was alone. The odor of coffee lingered.

On another occasion, while cuddling and feeling your warmth, I marveled again at your physicality and asked, "Can you hear and see me as a normal person would?" You answered cryptically but I read between the lines: *We dead don't want to be considered abnormal.* Once you became angry because I remarked how you looked better than before going to the hospital. Perhaps you were loath to recall past illness. Or maybe you didn't want to dispel the illusion (or reality) of your presence. In fact, whenever I noted that you were dead, the spell would shatter:

> I was with you at dawn today again,
> you so true-to-life
> that I knew beyond doubt
> you lived.
>
> When it dawned on me
> that you'd died,
> I took you aside
> for a serious talk.
> As usual, you clowned around,
> made out I was about
> to make an alarming confession.
> When I said, "Can you say
> what happened in May?"
> you let your tongue loll to the side
> in cartoon spoof of one who's died—
> and shocked me
> to tremble awake.

In one Dream a group of *caffè* cronies asked why you had been out of touch, to which you replied, rolling your eyes, *"Quando non si può, non si può!"* Accepting this vague excuse of your powerlessness, the friends wept, moved to have you back.

The ambiguity of your status comes out in many ways. In one Dream, in which we were on our way to a party, you said, "It's good I show my face."

> I knew it was because
> you'd gained the fame
> of being dead.
> I hugged and kissed you and
> you responded warmly,
> as in the old days.
> We reached downtown
> and you stepped inside a building.
> Shortly it occurred to me
> I would not see
> your face again.

Actually, many more visits were yet to come. And, in spite of your admonitions, I continue to question how you can be in the flesh in spite of your demise. In the beginning I rationalized that I had been mistaken, had gone to pick up your remains and found you alive. Once I told you, "American doctors underestimate the resilience of the Italian body." However, after some time, I began to deal with the paradox differently, toying with the idea that you could be both alive and dead. Even in Dreams I often recalled that your body was ashes, yet your presence was so incontrovertible that I would plan activities for us! You acknowledged your dual condition in a startling dream to Lynda, asking to attend her sewing classes because, you said, she knew how to cut fabric in two pieces and come up with two wholes. "Like me," you clarified: "one dead and one alive for Diane."

Usually I accept your dual nature readily but once I felt I was going mad entertaining two mutually exclusive realities. I told you so. You were in your thirties in that Dream and, when I looked beyond you to the other side of the bed, I saw a woman's figure lying there. It had long dark hair: my nineteen-seventy self. I grabbed the hair and lifted the body, light as a rag doll. It was a terrifying experience.

Perhaps embodying my "balancing acts," two identical Elios appear in a later dream, one on each side of me. At first I think there's a reflection but when I turn toward each figure it is definitely real. I embrace the Elio on my left, murmuring, "I want the sweet, the kind, the good."

Of all the explanations that I concocted to account for your survival, the most radical came in a typical Dream where you were indubitably real, I was sure I was awake, and yet I knew your body had been cremated. The only conclusion I could draw was that you had risen from your ashes like a Phoenix.

Occasionally, we discussed the conundrum. Amazed at how you recovered and admiring your renewed strength, I confessed my conviction that you died and cited evidence, such as the box of ashes: "*Ma la scatola di ceneri?*" On that occasion, you stopped hugging me and struck my brow with a light karate chop, at which point I awoke. I thought you delivered the chop to make me aware how divided my mind was—or was it a wakeup call to tell me I had broken the spell again?

Happily, you did not give up on me. A week later, you came in an extremely realistic Dream and we embraced. You were slim but bearded as in the late sixties. I exclaimed aloud, "But I'm wide awake!" You did not confirm or deny my statement. We made love.

Around this time, in my Dreams I began to sense that, although you were dead, you were available, not just in fleeting peak moments but continuously, and I thought how lucky I was to have you with me day after day. But I still had to ponder the discrepancy. Once I remarked, "It doesn't make sense." Then the Dream ended abruptly as Wakeful Dreams do when I question their incompatibility with daytime reality.

A year later I was still having such experiences and still trying to find a reasonable explanation for them, in my sleep. Once I asked you if friends would be able to see you next morning. You replied ambiguously that they might envision you. I tried to pin you down as to whether you had objective existence. I didn't doubt that you existed for me, but wanted to establish the extent to which you were real. No cogent explanation ever emerged.

As I prepared for swimming in Hawai'i and riding in France, I had a lovely Dream of you young, very handsome, with shiny gold-brown hair. We were lying in bed catching up and, when you heard of my plans, you were alarmed at how rigorous my activities would be—solicitous as always. I assured you that all would be fine, "now that death is behind us."

However, your death is not a closed case. In my Dreams you assume many aspects; you rally and flag and regain reality. Once, hearing your voice, I tracked down the sound and found a Black singer. Sometimes you shrink under my touch or morph into a different person, or I cannot make my eyes focus clearly on you. While making plans for our travels, I note you have no identity card: no death certificate. These are perturbing events, yet still I have some marvelous Dreams. Once, after hugging, kissing, and declaring my love, I asked if this was "true"; you confirmed that it was and also that it was a Dream. Another time, I interrupted intimacies to exclaim, "*È un sogno! Ci incontriamo nei sogni!*" You agreed, by smiling, laughing, and nodding, that indeed we meet in Dreams.

The theme of permanent presence recurs in Wakeful Dreams. Hearing workmen outside our window speaking in Roman dialect, you poke your head out and respond in kind. The familiar sound prompts me to comment, "*La vita è strana*": How strange life is, that you can be dead and yet I hear your voice every day! Another time, while stroking your head in my lap, I exclaim, "How lucky!" meaning, to have you with me always. I awake suddenly as usual, but there remains an after-image of your gleaming, sea-bright eyes.

Even nine and a half years after you dropped your physical body you resurrected it for me in a dream before dawn on what would have been your seventy-seventh birthday. You emerge from a group wearing a crisp blue custom-made Italian suit. You seem young but balding. When I cry, "Is it Elio?" you say, "Yes." Then I see you have a full head of hair. You are vividly present, radiant as in first youth. Your birthday gift to me!

Sometimes body and voice are lacking yet I recognize your presence. We dance, both of us disembodied, doing a fast shape-shift. As we zigzag riotously, it occurs to me that this is how spirits dance. Once again, although you are not apparent to the senses, I know you are with me. I feel cherished, secure, sure that you have been with me continuously. We are in complete harmony. I feel immense joy and relief that there is no longer cause for grief and am sure I can look forward to countless days with my companion. I run, skipping in ecstasy, gulping with each breath a substance that conveys delight. I know this charged air is addictive and I might be setting myself up for a fall. You could die again. I have adapted to your loss and now I am throwing that adaptation to the winds.

Once, after driving home from work, wishing I would find your soup on the table, I experience another poignant episode, this time of **Your Sympathy**:

> At last you'd come back
> into my dreams.
> I felt sure you'd stick around,
> that your absence
> had been an anomaly.
> I clasped your hand
> and cried, "*Non sarò più sola!*"
>
> Then I saw your face
> pinched with pity
> and knew you had to be
> on your way
> again.

So, *caro mio,* my Dreams of you come in many colors, from ecstatic recognition and certitude to wistfulness—and sometimes intense longing. Once, when an electric buzz alerted me that I was in the spirit realm, there—more than thirty years after his death—was that dear dog Tommy making a guest appearance in our bed, and

you were there too
but then you withdrew
and I flew after,
lifting off like a template
from my body flat on its back
and rocketing through space like that,
all the while wailing in desperation,
"Take me to where you are!"

On another occasion you co-starred with that other beloved dog José, dead for thirty-five years. Overwhelmed by the conviction that you and the dog had perpetual existence, I exclaimed: *"Paradiso!"*

My dreams have a couple of recurring themes or images. The most common is that of "twins." Sometimes the meaning seems clear, as when I choose to embrace "the sweet, the kind," or where you beg a friend to teach you how to be both dead and alive. But instances of twin animals and other phenomena crop up repeatedly in my sleep and even infiltrate my waking life, as the almost identical vases did at the bazaar. What do they mean? Do they ask me to accept the bad with the good, death with life? Perhaps they symbolize a wholeness or integration of two sides of the brain? I do not know, but sense they are significant. Recently a psychic, who did not know about my dreams, claimed you want to be reborn with me as twins! I'm not sure yet how I would feel about this.

Naturally, I have questioned the origin of my Wakeful and Lucid Dreams. I can see that they might reflect my desires and fears. One early Dream seemed clearly a wish-fulfillment, a bargaining for a period of grace. I was happy to spot you among the crowd and see you walk with vigor. I knew you had little time to live but was sure we'd share another Christmas.

Of course there are countless other dreams that are neither Wakeful nor Lucid and you figure in almost all of them. Your regular appearance by night no doubt is a compensation for your absence by day.

Phantom Limb

Often in dreams
you are there at my side
so near that I take you
for granted as in life:
a part of myself
I need not address
or even observe.
I know what you're up to,
how you feel.
After such a dream
there's nothing to remember.
I awake
and carry you about
with me
as always.

I sometimes drum up ideal scenarios, where you come as a
youth, bringing caresses and importunity, are kind to my parents,
tell me I am radiant. We sit at table and talk, with no TV. It seems
you want to make amends for neglectfulness and mend my mental
suffering.

In My Dreams

all that was rare
in our life
comes thronging:
consolation prizes—
psyche patches.

Wakeful Dreams can reflect a desperate desire to turn back
the clock and save you. In one such Dream I offer to read a manual
in techniques for self-healing,

but, typically, you reply
"Let me read it myself;
if you do, I'll be bored to death."
At this point I awake to the fact

death already closed its gate
and our plan for escape
was purely academic.

One rare Dream features a terrifying personification of death.

Grinning Reaper

We sit side by side in our living room while
the amiable Richard Dreyfus lookalike
hones his hacksaw.
He had intended to behead us
but settles on bobbing our feet.
I tell you in a stage whisper
to attack.
He doesn't seem to catch on
so you reach behind you
for a wrench.

Your feeble, ineffectual blow—
from an arm still maimed by the stroke—
makes no dent
in our beguiling executioner.

If I catch rightly
the drift of this Dream,
the dead can't help the living
to evade the smiling slasher.

Echoing an early perception of death as a kidnapper, I
dreamed once that you and I had entered an unfamiliar house,
whereupon an Asian man, a stranger, hustled you into the base-
ment, ignoring me. I ran around to the back, hoping to glimpse
you. In fact, you were sitting on a cot close to a large window with
only a flimsy, torn screen separating us. However, you made no
move to escape and said they would treat you better if I was not
bossing you around. I awoke, shocked at the rebuff, and pondered
all day what the Dream might signify. It seems you were telling me
you are irrevocably in the Underworld. Perhaps I saw your keeper
as an Asian because I read *The Tibetan Book of the Dead* aloud to

you after you died. And perhaps you will suffer fewer conflicts if I stop pushing you to visit.

Despite this apparent message, I continue to hope for more Wakeful Dreams. When there is a hiatus, I lament that my dreams have gone blind, the nights of my life lost to darkness. It's the old fear, of losing you and having no recourse, no way to make contact. The terror has attenuated in time, but so have the vivid Dreams. To think you may stop visiting leaves me with an empty, incomplete feeling.

I like to review the Dreams that don't reflect my wants or fears, Dreams that must have been initiated by you. An early one comes back like a refrain. In it you stayed with me for quite a while. I was delighted to be a widow no longer, sure that we'd done the right thing to bring you home from the hospital.

> Suddenly, out of the blue,
> with customary sarcasm, you said,
> "Do I have to send a telegram?"

Then I awoke, a widow once more, still curious to know what the obvious fact was that, because of my denseness, I had to decipher from a "telegram."

Are you frustrated because you attended your memorial and sent the meditating cat, the tarnished coin, the hawks, the twin vases, and still I keep crying, "Where are you"? The "telegram" is delivered repeatedly, I suppose, in Signs and significant Dreams.

On the other hand, I sometimes wonder if I am concocting Dreams from scraps of past experience and hopes. One wish-ful-filler, which I concluded nonetheless was initiated by you, found us dancing as in courtship times, joyously, with many improvisations on your part—our **Last Tango**:

> I was at a high-country retreat
> when you came in a Dream,
> young and clean-shaven.
>
> You put a slow tango on the hi-fi
> and we danced body to body.
> I don't think we spoke.

I just smiled and savored you,
brushing your cheek with my lips
as we sailed zestfully about.

I marveled at how alive you were
and could see that your chances
of beating cancer were good.

Then I woke up and recalled
that you had aged and died.
But my dismay was allayed

by the thought that you'd come
young to bring a bit of happiness
and leave a good last impression.

The Dreams that seem most clearly to be your idea are the
ones where you haunt me as a **Sexy Ghost:**

It seems unlikely
that at this point
I would conjure in dream
your young body
bold and virile
as it comes to me often
so real that I can feel
the silky hair on your chest,
a lean cage on which I lean.
Would I re-invent
such intimacies
as we shared
in a distant past?

I believe, instead,
it is you
who transcend time
and flit at will
to choose
morning kisses,
night-time thrills.

I will probably never know whether Signs and Dreams come from you and if you share my experiences, as it seems. However, the fact that I never had a psychic experience before—and never dreamed of you as younger while you lived—makes me think that some agent beyond my own mind is in play.

Chapter 6
Ceremonies

Ritual at Stuart Fork

I sift your ashes
through my hands,
silky but for
fragments
of bone.

After offerings and incense
I heap your dust
among flowers on a cloth
and loose it in the stream.
A cloud of blue-gray
blooms in emerald water.
Some chips sink,
pale pebbles
by the ivory quartz that
cross-hatches the boulder
where you bent to fish.

How can I reconcile
these relics
with the memory of you
in red bandanna
casting and questioning
inscrutable waters?

SIGNS AND DREAMS COME of their own accord, but Ceremonies I must perform. Some are for you, some for me, and some for both of us. In all cases the aim is the same: transcendence, equanimity. Ceremony transforms suffering and lack into peace and plenty, sometimes by a simple supplication:

> May I enter emptiness
> silent, open, as into a sanctum
> and attain to that profound calm
> wherein all losses are re-found.

I take what measures I can to mend my brokenness. But what can I do for you? Death is an all-important transition. While you were dying I followed the scant directions I had been exposed to. Tibetan monks say that the dying person requires a calm environment, so I held back from weeping at your bedside, sometimes pacing hospital corridors gritting my teeth to keep from crying out. When I brought audio tapes of lamas describing what to expect at the crucial juncture, you listened but said there was too much to absorb. Nonetheless, I hope that whatever you could catch was helpful. At the last moment you opened your eyes and looked upward; I like to think you made a clean departure through the crown *chakra*, as yogis say one should.

We had no connections with chaplains and I did not try to procure one for you. However, one came to my aid impromptu as I took my break on the day of your death. I don't know why I left your side, since I was quite sure you were about to die. I probably hoped you'd slip away when I wasn't looking. Anyway, as usual, I couldn't remember where I left my car in the five-story hospital parking garage. At the top, under the sun, I came across a gray-haired Black man washing a car. I commented on this, we struck up a conversation, and I told him about you. Before helping me locate my car, he prayed for us. The card he left said he was pastor of a certain church.

Next day I unearthed the card
of that benevolent apparition
who had seized my hands
in a faltering moment
and prayed strength into me.
In fact I drove past his church,
just to be sure it stood foursquare
on this earthly plane.

Silvia had stayed with you while I was out. When I came back
she said you had not stirred. You were on a morphine drip. We
stood on either side of your bed, chatting and joking until you
opened your eyes and I said, "Hi." You did not reply. We both
watched as you looked up, cheeks puffed, and subsided quietly,
closing your eyes for the last time. Silvia said, "*Vaya con Dios.*" She
would have lingered longer, but I encouraged her to leave.

It was tremendous for me to see you release your last breath,
returning what you had borrowed from the great pool of air we
all share. However, I refrained from touching your body, as the
lamas advise, for this is not a moment to indulge in attachments.
I read passages from *The Tibetan Book of the Dead* that exhort the
newly deceased to be aware of their state and to stay with the initial
brilliant light and serene emptiness that they experience. After
the reading, I sat by your bed and meditated. I did not look at
you or touch you. I had asked the hospital staff to give us privacy.
However, a bouquet arrived for you from Ingrid; she did not know
you would not see it. Or did you?

While on break I had phoned Lynda and Carlo, who were
still sending get-well cards. Hearing that you were on the brink
of death, they dropped everything and rushed down from Grass
Valley. They arrived at the hospital at three-thirty, about two hours
after you died. When a nurse told them you'd passed, they were
a bit apprehensive about viewing your body. They told me later
how relieved they were to see you looking peaceful. Lynda said you
seemed asleep. We called the undertakers but did not wait for them
to reach the hospital. We drove together to the bayside trail that
you and I frequented, at that moment a sort of sacred space, and

walked. We had dinner at your favorite grill and bar, and drank to you. Then the two of them kept me company during the night, all of us sleeping on recliners in the living room. This unprecedented slumber party served the purpose of a wake, although your body was not in attendance. Thus my friends ferried me through the first period of being alone. A few days later Roxanne and Jon came bringing lunch for us to share, an old Jewish custom. These acts of kindness were themselves a kind of sacrament honoring you and comforting me.

The first morning, after Lynda and Carlo left, cold shivers beset me. I was not sick and the May day was dawning sunny and warm. Was I feeling this ague because your body was in the under-taker's refrigerator? Tibetans claim the spirit may take a few days to detach from the physical form. I felt some alarm, imagining your confusion, and said aloud, "You have dropped your body!"

In the following days, as you requested, I sat where you used to sit and read aloud passages from the Tibetan book that describes hallucinations one can expect each day following death: the visions of the *bardos* between incarnations. For a non-Buddhist you certainly dog-eared that sacred text! I had not realized how often you re-read it. There is nothing in Christianity or Judaism to compare with Tibetan Buddhism, so detailed in description of the dying process and what one will see in the afterlife. It also gives instructions for what to do about it. I'm amazed—and pleased—at how lucid you were in your last days, and how provident, to ask that I read these texts to you after death.

The *bardos*, I realized as I read each day, present a devolving situation. It is virtually assumed that you will fail to remain in the first sublime light. The apparitions become increasingly scary and, of course, they are typically Tibetan. I injected a few qualifications as I read through these bizarre descriptions, saying that you might be seeing something else from western mythology—or of your own invention. However, the important point, reiterated after each *bardo*, is valid for everyone: Be aware that all images are projections of your mind; once you own them, you will stop being afraid—and may still have a chance at awesome emptiness.

From another Tibetan source I discovered the *phowa*, a ceremony which you probably did not know about. It is called a rite for "transference of consciousness" and is recited as if from the deceased's point of view. It is supposed to induce compassion in you and conjures a spiritual role model from which healing rays of forgiveness and love expand. I performed a *phowa* daily for you during the first few months, suggesting that you envision our preceptor, Maharishi, as your model of compassion. In the presence of that radiant Transcendental guru, we not only learned how to teach meditation, but how to appreciate each other more deeply.

On special occasions I perform a *puja* with flowers, incense, and fruit offerings. I miss the sound of your deep voice intoning the Sanskrit by my side. It is a Ceremony that induces tranquility; and I trust it brings you peace as I perform it. One thing that bothers me is my failure to remind you to think your mantra at the last moment. We knew from experience that meditation opens us to a sublime emptiness and Maharishi recommended that we meditate as death approaches. Perhaps you remembered without my prompting.

Having only tenuous connections to sacred traditions, I have improvised expressions of my own for my solace and yours. Occasionally a poem will come out in the form of a prayer:

Godspeed

As the tide in full flow
lifts the two-prowed canoes
up and over the reefs
and speeds them to high seas,
so may the surge that overflows
from friends' hearts
propel you toward the ocean
of everlasting bliss.

I never seem able to think on my feet—unlike you—and feel dissatisfied with the scant praise I pronounced in front of friends at the original memorial and on the anniversaries. A need to honor you formally was pressing on me, so I've written a tribute in my journal, a sort of private obituary for you. I prefaced it with recollection of your many identities from youth to age and your many moods from acerbic to mellow,

> but under all your guises I sense an essential you who is
> sweet, humorous (even at your own expense), warm,
> courageous, caring, resourceful, provident, talented,
> strong, sexy, above all tender toward animals.
> If I should discover you reborn, it will be by these traits
> that I will recognize you. This essential you was not always
> expressed but I always knew it was there and always loved it.

Occasionally I re-read get-well and sympathy cards, and the Lorca poem about the "unique coin," which Christina read at your memorial. In the early days I frequently took comfort in the lines you wrote to yourself, that **Posthumous Message**:

> How fortuitous that I should find
> that card with the Phoenix on it
> in time to read the message
> at your memorial.
> I've propped up that image
> with its widespread red wings
> and egg-gripping talons
> on top of the box
> that holds your ashes.
> Once in a while I read it aloud
> to remind myself, as well as you,
> that this clay is not
> the essential You

Being attentive to significant artifacts is a sort of ritual. Once while cleaning the house my heart contracted and sank as I dusted the box holding your dust but rebounded when

> I met the aqua gaze of the eyes
> in the silver head you made,
> which resembles you so much,
> fire glowing from the opal in its brow—
> your focus at point of death.

Music is another great healer. After you died I felt a soreness around my heart because you listened to so few of the many CDs you collected and you will never enjoy the fruit of your efforts. I also felt it would be ungrateful not to accept your largesse. So I listened to your music, methodically playing a few CDs per day until I heard them all, weeping as I listened to *soleares*, the sound of loneliness. Most pieces lifted my spirits.

Interface

I drank a glass of wine
and listened to
the long-winded, lilting
lyrical cello sonatas
of Bach.
The whole house rang
with their singing.
Even as I lamented
the loss of you
my longing was leavened
with the lingering notes
and almost phased
into joy.

In church I cry often, from both happiness and the poignancy of your loss. Yes, after some fifty years of abstention, I go to church. Guess where? Jocelyn and Peter enjoyed a Christmas Eve program at a local non-denominational church and persuaded me to give it a try. It was Northbrae, where we were married! Do you remember the resplendent abstract rainbows in stained glass fore and aft and the side panels representing Lao-tzu, Muhammad, and Gandhi, as well as biblical characters? Besides hymns there are old masses and other classical pieces. At first I felt a twinge, imagining your baritone complementing the splendid tenor in the choir. Although your absence overwhelms me at times, I am moved to profound gratitude for this niche after my long alienation from conventional religion. Here no exclusive creed is recited. It seems almost a Sign that this church happens to be the site of our marriage. I am reminded of T.S. Eliot's lines in *Four Quartets*: "We shall not cease from exploration/And the end of all our exploring/Will be to arrive where we started/And know the place for the first time."

Shortly after you died Franco gave me a pamphlet by Yogananda. It provides rites for communicating with the dead. I doubt that I am evolved enough to do them effectively, but I've tried and have been moved, hoping you were communicating silently, as it seemed, when I performed these **Ceremonies**:

> As usual, on the weekly anniversary
> of your passing away
> I performed a *puja* and a *phowa* ceremony
> and then I meditated.
> In the stillness I envisioned you
> as Yogananda says to do
> in the third eye raised between the other two.
> I sent you all my love and pardon
> for all the pain you had occasioned,
> assuring you that it came not from sin,
> as Padre Pio defines it, but weakness.
> Then I pictured you responding.
> Within my heart you smiled and wept
> and I joined in, blending tears
> of wordless cherishing and gratitude.

I also invented a ritual to free myself of anger and help me forgive your trespasses. I wrote all the hurtful words of criticism that you used to repeat and then sent them away in flames on a kitchen burner. I've had a few relapses since then, but not many. Nonetheless, I hope you also have a means of exorcism and are rid of bad old habits.

Another intuition of posthumous reconciliation came while I was in retreat at Cobb Mountain. With the rarefied atmosphere and extra meditations, I was more sensitive than usual and had a strong sense of **Merger** with you:

> In reverie
> you spoke from the heart of me
> where the great sage
> said you'd be,

smiling familiarly,
to assure
that you're there
at my core,
not gone forever.
You brighten
when I welcome you
with praise and fond memories
and blend into my being.
Then we dance to one melody.
My life gives life to you
and you enliven me.

I have mentioned my habit of toasting you at mealtime and telling you what I'm eating. It's a way to include you and evoke your presence. I also set up an altar for *Día de los muertos*. It is an early Mesoamerican rite that has survived into post-Columbian times. Actually it is more like a week rather than just a day to invite the dead to visit. I used to enjoy the make-believe of Halloween, but now I appreciate its holy aspect as the season when the departed have access to earthly haunts. So I borrow the ancient tradition by placing your photo with mom's, dad's, Jean's, Nino's, and the dogs' on the sideboard in the dining room with candles and the loved ones' favorite things. I offer the dogs some kibble—and was galvanized one morning to see that Kipper's had been consumed, every crumb neatly eaten with no surrounding mess! This happened twice. I saw no sign of cat or mouse, but decided to blame the opportunistic Siamese from across the street. I don't want to slip too far into superstition. For you I put out wine and bread, your hiking stick and a hat. None of these disappeared.

Memento Mori

There it is, spread out
with flowers, incense,
votives and libations
before each likeness:
my altar for
Day of the Dead.

Nine faces smile,
confident, pensive,
enthusiastic, benign—
so real, so *here*
it is hard to believe
you are the *disappeared*.

When I contemplate your images, I feel camaraderie as I would with guests and try to divine how you felt and feel. Your familiar faces communicate a certain assurance:

How was it for you, I wonder,
to take the final step.
Were you prepared,
surprised, appalled?
Your faces never cease to smile,
alluring, assuaging the fear
of my own ineluctable leap.

On May 14 I hold a memorial dinner with your closest friends. It tides me over the anniversary and also welcomes you into our midst. The first year I drew a large *mandala* with pastel pencils on black paper. It shows five Phoenixes flying forth from a flaming matrix formed by their tails in the center. They pass through a circular spectrum, their bodies a fiery red, their fierce beaks piercing the void beyond. Under it I posted a copy of the words you wrote inside your Phoenix card: "a reminder/That after the fire has consumed the gross matter/That creates flames, that belongs to this plane,/Only the Self shall be." The Phoenix *mandala* has assumed the aspect of a sacred object hanging on my wall to remind me of transcendence.

One year, when I had consulted a medium, the friends all held hands at table and waited for you to move a light object— a feather—as you promised via the medium that you would try to do. It seemed nothing happened, but later one of the women confided that she perceived a rainbow ball of energy circulating among us, radiating joy and stopping only when it reached a guest who expressed incredulity about an afterlife.

After some years I began to feel that I should not keep your ashes forever closed in a box. I watched for a Sign or Dream that would tell me when and where to disperse them, but no message came through. When I was packing for my trip to the Trinity Alps, it occurred to me that at least some of the ashes should go back to the place that you loved most of all. Near the big boulder by the favorite campground I found a flat rock or ledge, on which I set up the objects for a *puja*. After the little Ceremony, I gathered the flowers used in it onto the red bandanna altar cloth, together with your ashes, and swished them in the clean green water. The ritual was beautiful and elevating, the cloud of ashes dispelled in the current evocative of our bodies' ultimate union with the elements. However, a few pale pellets—of bone or teeth, I suppose—sank in a line. I stared and stared at them, so unlike the image sharp in memory of you leaning into your cast, standing on the cross-hatched declivity that spring freshets had scoured in the big rock. I remember how the filament caught sunlight filtering through tall cedars and how the fly bristled on the current while we conjured rainbow trout to rise out of the emerald depths.

Another handful of ashes is buried under our rosemary bush, *for remembrance*, and some are on the bayside trail under a windswept acacia that produces sunny blooms in spring. I cast the fourth batch to the sky at Marin Headlands, **On Old Springs Trail:**

> Fistful by fistful,
> my back to a lichened rock,
> I give the last of
> your ashes to the air.
> Wind from the sea below
> and the sun above
> dance with your dust
> till it settles down
> to roots of poppy and lupine.
> I hear the crows call
> and the small water gush.
> I remember where you stood
> and how your shadow fell
> where hare and hawk convene.

I close my eyes
on starting tears
and feel the sun darken.
Then out of the blue
the sky too weeps.

The sublime and the ridiculous rub shoulders so frequently,
you have to figure the Creator has a sense of humor. In March, for
my birthday, Kris and Nick take me for a walk in the headlands,
culminating in a wine-infused picnic at the lichen-covered rock
where I performed my private scattering Ceremony. The first time
we sat there Nick wanted to know whether this was a case of "asses
to ashes and duffs to dust." How you would have laughed! Perhaps
you did, and perhaps you sent the hawk who loitered over our pic-
nic while haze gathered to ring the sun with an opalescent halo: an
exact reproduction of the Sign that came on your cremation day!

Laughter, tears, awe! They alternate to massage the psyche
recovering from trauma. In fact, my moods shift mercurially from
one to the other, like the skies of Kauai, where rain and shine con-
stantly play counterpoint. With Ceremonies I put reverence into
the mix. Often the gods of nature provide ritual enough. From the
window of my red and gold room in Provence, I witnessed the rites
of trees.

Cypresses in Provence

You called them pointed trees,
these guardians of lanes
and hallowed ground.
Sweetly they sway
in the southern breeze.
They dance like Shiva
with a thousand limbs
tucked close, loose a few
to the soft wind's whims.

They survey horses
hock-high in summer hay,
hear spring waters dripping down.
They count the hours of passing life
and wisely nod their fragile crowns.

A bittersweet sensation arose from seeing vibrant horses under those funeral *alberi pizzuti,* as you called them. And yet those trees dance like gods and acquiesce, it seems, to mortality—an emblem of equanimity in the face of life and death.

Postscript

LOOKING BACK ON MY JOURNEY through disorienting vertigo, disconcerting searches, wavering verdicts—and on to cherished Signs, Dreams, Ceremonies—I could conclude that I am obsessed with a search for something I will never have again. In a way this is true, of course. However, there is another way to view loss and recovery. It comes from questioning *what* it is we yearn for when we miss a beloved person. Maharishi, our meditation teacher, once said with a mischievous giggle, "Strangely enough, we love only the Self." Of course he meant the upper case Self that Elio referred to in his card—a Self that is neither I nor he nor you, but a pervasive essence. When we glimpse this essence in another person we fall in love. It produces a glow that redeems his negative traits. If we lose sight of it, we fall out of love and wonder what we ever saw in him. Although at times disillusioned, I never fell out of love with Elio. I sense that we share one Self and that it outlasts the dropping of the body.

Peace like a River

Trinity branch, our vacation home,
a stream of many mansions:
High strait corridors echo,
engorged with gushing day-melt;
willow-filled vestibules riffle with
chirps of backwash and warbler;
tall walls papered in cedar, redwoods,
and firs upright as godly doormen
guard glass-floored sunrooms;
in rumpus, rocks round from torrents,
gold-varnished, speckled as trout sides,
churn and toss back the flux, juggle
drops you transfixed with film on high,
poised in the manner of Hokusai.

Below the shed-size boulder lies
the basin and basement of repose:
emerald pool, its threshold cross-hatched
in quartz, deer route and drinking ford—
my launch-pad to swim, yours to cast a line—
and the sublime unsounded depth itself,
stirred barely by faint flick of fish.

I consigned a handful of your dust
to that sink of the silent world
and it spread like a nebula
gray in the green suspended
as in unmoving heaven.
Then slowly it drifted away
on the imperceptible current—
proof that no stasis is perfect
in the realm of floods and freshets.

The Poems

AFTER ELIO DIED I wrote over three hundred poems for him. Some have appeared in their entirety. Others were quoted in part within the context of a journal message. For poetry enthusiasts, I include here the full text of poems excerpted or merely adumbrated in the prose sections.

Chapter 1: Vertigo

On Old Quarry Trail

On this summer day
that you do not see
I walk an ascending path
between dry weeds
pausing in the shade,
as we used to do,
to search shadows and wind
for some trace of you.
I climb at last to an overview
of a mountain in the depths.

Among those hills and valleys
and in the whole broad world
you are not here.
This news borne by the breeze
chills and bruises my heart.

~

Clearance

When the great sale finally took place
I woke up dizzy and sick,
afraid I wouldn't make the clearance.
Friends thought I'd brought on the spell
because I was about to sell all your stuff.
I did feel rotten putting up your backpack,
thinking of all those years
when you'd hoisted it above the bears
on a pulley system you'd devised
(still there in a pocket on one side).
Finally, I was reconciled to the state of affairs
and tore into the job of unloading your endless
and frequently duplicate or triplicate
supplies of tools, light meters, and glasses,
not to mention the unmentionable
decorative items from thrift stores
and the big, useless, cumbersome stuff
like your exercise machine,
the distiller, and the synthesizer.
By the time I'd lugged it all out
and boxed the small items,
prevailing on friends to price
the cameras and power tools,
I was fed up and angry at you
for putting us all through all that.
For the first time I didn't miss you.
I was just wrapped up
in unloading as much as I could.
There was still plenty left over
to be sorted, sold, or given away.
My neighbor says it will take a year—
and maybe I'll stay mad even longer.

Be it as it may, I missed you again today.

It seems I still love you as always,
"in spite of everything,"
as we always used to say.

∼

Freakish Finality

Although I know death's a fact of life
and I've seen many go before you,
your death still leaves me incredulous.
It seems outrageous and anomalous—
an improper, impetuous act
that sadly you cannot retract.

∼

Seasons of the Sea

On the ocean of grief
swells of sorrow
strike broadside,
memories swamp,
sobs dance like dinghies
on choppy seas.
I sink beyond my depth.

Still, in a moment of calm
I sense I am immersed
in the Element
that buoys all.

∼

Just Checking

From time to time, while I cook or read,
I pause and mutter words I dread:
"He won't be coming home; he's dead."
Of course I do not need a reminder.
I test my strength against this sentence
as one tries limbs sapped by confinement.
I check for reprieve when I'll breathe free
and these words no more
knock the wind out of me.

~

Swift Kick

I've been kicked out of complacency,
booted from banality.
I rebound from inertia
with the stinging spring of pain.
Gone is the reticence,
the fear of faux-pas.
I am bold, I step forth.
The walls that kept me cloistered
are crumbling with my tears.
Resentments rankling for years
are forgiven, almost forgotten.
Death-begotten fears
hold less dread
since you have gone ahead.

Because it shunts me
from passivity,
I pay tribute to your death,
tough lover.

~

The Best of Times

One hears of barbarians
who burn the bereaved wife
or execute and entomb her
with the family jewels.
But I am civilized
and have a life of my own.
I carry on my career
and your chores too.
I am increased, not diminished,
by your demise.
I survive.
Why then do my thoughts
willfully inter themselves
in the room where you died
and in the little box
that holds your dust?

~

Day Break

At dawn when I awake to your loss
I smart anew from pangs of separation
like a baby cast up
from the amniotic sea
onto the lonely isle of selfhood.
Just so I am birthed each day
from amorphous nights of dreams
where you are still afloat
to face the dawn of exile.

~

Dragline

I dash about with my usual verve
rehearsing explanations
for points of grammar
or menus for meals with friends.
As always I walk fast and feel
as if I'm getting somewhere.
Then I recall that you're not here
and wonder why I rush
as if looking forward
to one of our walks
or dinner together.
There is no need to hurry
unless, perhaps, I expect
to meet you at
the end of the line.

I slacken my pace,
amazed how a lack
can feel so heavy.

∼

April Fools

On April One, Two Thousand and Two
you went with no undue
alarm to keep your date
with the CT scan.
We didn't worry until we learned
a tumor in your brain
had prompted a hemorrhage—
and that was why your right side
didn't work too well.
Your blood was way too thin,
ready to cause another stroke.

If thickened too much,
it could clot in your heart.
We seemed to be the butt
of a perfect prank.
Nonetheless, you did not succumb
but went on to radiation therapy,
growing weaker each day.
By the time we learned the cause—
an infection caught in hospital—
you were too far gone to rally.
The cancer in your lung
had free rein then.
They gave you days to live.
That was the punch line.

~

Final Photos

They seemed the epitome of sadness,
you looking straight into the lens,
an eyebeam faint but fully aware
that you were about to leave
me and this world forever.
Your eyes, on verge of weeping,
said farewell
with all your heart.

A friend said he saw
only your great debilitation.
I looked again without trepidation,
perceiving less sorrow now.
In one frame I made out a little smile.
However, it was a smile
that said a wan good-bye.

~

One Thing I Could Not Do

was gaze upon you afterward;
kiss your pale, unfeeling brow;
stroke your numb, cooling hand.
I could not look in the face
you used to wear
knowing you were not there.

Did I forego good-bye
because you had
already gone—
or did I guess
we'd meet again?

~

Cremation

I linger on your lower lip,
luscious, youthful;
peruse the rascally sprigs
that elude containment by your hat;
recall your strong, supple palms
adept at crafts and caresses.
Your eyes, forget-me-not blue,
could turn to ice in anger
or melt in amusement.

They melted indeed
the day your body was burned—
fragile jellies in the furnace.
The little hairs cringed first,
disappeared in the rush of flame.
Even your trunk charred,
shuddered, collapsed.

The bag of ashes they gave me
bore no resemblance
to the you I knew,
sweet as a sun-kissed fig.

Can I be blamed if
I return again and again
to pluck forbidden fruit
from the fire?

~

Out of Sight

Can it be the weight
of years to come
or memories
that crowd my chest?

Perhaps it's the thousand days
since you died
that gather like snow
to crush a roof.

All I know is that
in an unexamined spot—
the dark side of the moon—
something mutely quakes.

~

Forging Fortitude

A weathering occurs
as meditation takes turns
with monsoons of sorrow.
Sizzling downpours drown

in dispassionate depths of mind
and disappear.
At times the hot tears flow
even while serenity prevails,
tropic rains
coating cool windowpanes.
These shifts
from agitated heat
to dousing cold
temper endurance
fold on fold.

∽

Chapter 2: Where Are You?

Weather Too Fair

It's another rare day
with early morning sunshine—
weather we used to welcome
for walks, the beach, wash on the line.
The ten days you lay dying
were also most beautiful—
like the scene in a Japanese film
where noble men commit ritual suicide
while pink plum petals fall
from a sky celestially calm:
such loveliness
from which they—like you—
were wrenched!

∽

When Freesias Bloom

once more
yellow, white, and red,
a year will have sped by
since you gazed
amazed at them
through the window
in the door.
Can it be
that you took
with you
some memory
of them
and me?

~

Wild Fennel

Today I was taken off guard,
walking alone on our bayside trail,
by the pungent licorice smell
of many man-high fennels.
Green and gold, they throng the way,
witnesses to our wanderings:
a suitable setting for a picture
you might take of me,
relaxed and smiling because
I walk with you.

~

Ex-Communion

The Host is invoked,
the wine is poured.
With whom will I
break bread, make a toast?

I have no companion
with whom to clink a glass
over the bounty of the land.
This quasi sacrament
meant for sharing
makes my solitary supper
an almost sacrilege.

~

Closing the Curtains

A signal that day is done,
time to turn up the heat
or light a fire
and be cozy
at home.

A gesture so simple yet defined,
to pull a cord
and close out
the coldness
beyond.

An action at each day's end
that marked the hour
when you and I
would settle in
together.

A ritual whose meaning is reversed,
to signify your absence
from this house,
my enclosure here
alone.

~

Peaches

At times in the little Chinese market
you can find huge, juicy peaches
like the one I was eating in Rome
that morning when you came
to pick me up at my room.
We didn't imagine on that first date
we'd spend so many years together
and that I'd be weeping today
because nothing remains of us
but memories
and so many reminders
like this enormous peach
that I hold in my hand.

~

Pursuit

The wind routes its rounds,
frisks each leaf and grass blade,
looking for something.
Perhaps it has heard
you're a missing person.
My mind rides with it,
restlessly calling,
"Where are you?"

Perhaps you have stopped
in a pocket of calm
where we have no warrant
to follow. Yet I hope
you will come forth
and turn yourself in.

~

I Thought I Knew You

Through forty years I acquired
a sense of what pleases you
or draws your scorn.
I could predict what you
were about to say,
how you would want
to spend an evening.
I could foresee your rapture
as favorite music tuned in,
your smile of amusement
at antics of animals
or favorite jokes.

Now I have no idea
what you feel. I wonder
if you are homesick—
or if the afterlife offers
fantastic attractions.
I wish to know
that you can hear me
and see that I miss you.

Like death itself,
you are a mystery.
I am at a loss

even to imagine
who, or what, or if
you are.

～

Dream Lands

When we meet in dreams
great gurus would claim
it is within the astral plane.
When I awake and
you fade like a phantom
perhaps you return to that domain.

Sometimes I think you're dreaming of me,
causing my flesh to shiver.
When you re-awake in your world
do details dissolve in your light
and memories melt in your day?

～

Your Hats

They still hang on a rack by the door:
the ruby beret, mate to my scarlet one,
our signature attire for winter walks;
your cotton cloche worn in the wheelchair
before and after radiation to the brain;
the canvas shade-maker laced against wind;
and that translucent safari helmet
that bathed your face with filtered gold.
You went off without your hats!
What were you thinking?

～

Surprise Ending

Images of you flash before me,
stills from a film forty years long—
feature length.
I discern you dimly, slim and brown,
in moccasins among Rome traffic
sidestepping like a young matador.
In a later action shot, swashbuckling,
you leap California river rocks,
calibrating momentum, angle, slickness.
One frame stands out with happy clarity
where you caper to Peruvian pipes.
For performances in the kitchen
you wear an apron to knead, de-seed,
stir, taste, and deliver tidbits
for my delectation and appreciative guests.
Then you sit with glass raised
jauntily to click with ours. Film rolls.
The cloud-streaked scenes on Hanalei Bay
show you in shorts and your safari hat.
Your red beret and green vest flare as
you wheel to the curb to give me a ride and,
in the next scene, wait in the wheelchair
for me to pick you up.

Suddenly frames flicker fast forward:
you stuck in your seat too weak to move,
then clamped to an air mask,
your once robust right arm
trembling, needle-stuck.
You breathe your last and instantly
color fades from the image of your face.
No voice-over announces
the unspeakable process
that reduces your beloved body

to a fistful of ashes, leaving
this viewer bewildered
at how any movie
could end like that.

~

Clips

After you departed I stared
in shock at your empty chair.
Then memories welled up
of you clean-shaven, young and thin,
gray-bearded, and phases in between:
solemn youthful gaze that crazed
like a glaze and cracked into giggles;
prime-age limber legs poised
to leap between river rocks;
smart-ass mug that precluded
any chance of candid shots;
elder glance askance with grin
at off-camera jokester.
Images so convincing
that my loss multiplied
as I scanned them.

I was wrong to screen your life in shards.
It was a subtly mutating continuum,
a filmstrip unwound to reach completion.
Still I cut and edit stills
to assuage my craving for re-runs.

~

The Ever Present

"It seems only yesterday" rings true
as I thumb through old snaps
of Dad rapt by the dolphin show,
near and real as Mom,
who survived him by a score.

You, more vivid yet, appear
shifting shape from year to year.
You gaze in my face at the altar
and waves of romance overwhelm me—
so many years a flimsy fence
washed out by waters of remembrance.
You fish in Stuart Creek
and countless summers return with
resinous breezes and glittering pines.
Your laughing likeness floats back
the punch line of a wisecrack.

Memory keeps no calendar.
Twenty years from now
in the trackless time
of my deep mind
you'll be alive as ever.

~

How the Garden Grows

Remember the lantana bitten by frost?
It's flared up like a flame again,
red and gold, colors of Rome and Spain.
Also, the hibiscus procured in Hawai'i
as a bit of a stick is hanging on to life.
Your thyme and dwarf laurel
spread their resinous smell,

and outside the kitchen window
your little potted rose
raises its piquant red buds.
Tomatoes grow like Jack's beanstalk
as they always did for you—
and I see you lean
to tie them on racks,
clip sprigs of aromatic herbs,
toss weeds into a bin.
One thing about the deceased:
You don't deviate from old routines.

~

Smelling the Coffee

Except for our courtship times,
I could never quite savor
the full-bodied you,
a rich blend always brewing.
You poured yourself
into work, pastimes, pals.
I was there by your side,
probably preoccupied
with other matters—
but taking in your emanations
as one inhales the aroma
of coffee, almost better
than the sip itself.
The essence of you—
cordial, tender, brave—
pervaded our daily rounds
and lingers,
evoking your presence
like a fragrance
even now.

~

Coming to Terms

(with a nod to Dostoevsky and Nisargadatta Maharaj)

How futile to think:
what if doctors had caught on
to the invasion by infection
in time to stem its onslaught?
You might have lived
for who knows how long
with chemotherapy and radiation.
I am tempted to say that fate
caused the doctors to drop the ball:
fate—shorthand for the fact
that we are all responsible for all,
no result with one cause only,
everything always involved.
Complication foils prediction.

I know this is so
but instinct impels me
to envision a hinge
where destiny's door
swings the other way
and you are still here.

~

Life is But a Dream

Even in youth you saw
this world and all of us
as parts of one being.
We later learned

some give this entity
the aspect of a god,
perhaps Mother Divine,
or simply an invisible
all-informing Intelligence
that dreams us into existence.
We are, it is said, that
and nothing but that.
What happens, I wonder,
when that Great Mind
awakens, as it has in your case,
from the dream of our singular self?
For you now the answer
is either obvious or irrelevant.
For me—still dreamt but bereft
of the figment that was you—
to know is of the essence.

∽

Chapter 3: Balancing Acts

When the Trickster Retires

You'd never wear suspenders to work.
After playing too many practical jokes,
you feared fillips in return.
You had a passel of pranks
to play on me: ambush cat-fashion
or barrage of hand-rubbed sparks
delivered in mock heroic manner.

In time, your tally of tricks trickled away.
When the jester no longer stepped forth,
death found the coast clear
to step in.

~

Great Adventure

As you lay dying you queried,
"Who knows what it will be like?"
I quoted the poet Neihardt,
who said he felt no dread of death.
"It will be a great adventure," he claimed,
confident he'd see his son and long-gone wife.
You appeared satisfied with the poet's prediction,
but I wonder if it proved true for you
who were so involved with domestic life.
In your mouth the word "home"
had a sacramental sound.
Were you able, on such short notice,
to drop attachment to equipment selected
for crafts and cooking and rare carpet repair,
not to mention your collection
of great music and books?
What a shift it must have been
to launch into the void
bereft of all your things,
even your body,
and take on
that great adventure!

~

Days of Judgment

I seem bent on trying our marriage.
Was it a happy one or not?
There's negative evidence in exhibit A:
those marriage encounter letters
where I introduce concrete complaints

and you remain mainly vague
and baselessly optimistic.

On further deliberation, however,
I must admit circumstantial evidence
of mutual enrichment.
The clues are all around me
in this house adorned with our artwork
and mementos of our trips.

Also, I cannot deny
I rejoiced in your enjoyment
(of certain things)
more than in my own.
While we weigh the *quid pro quo*s
let's add to the record
that your presence was a magnet
that drew my love into existence.

There are reasonable doubts,
making for a hung jury.
Perhaps it's best to give up
on reaching a verdict.

~

Big Bang

I supposed I would not suppress
such a thing as a fractured self.
But I did
until you died
and blew the lid
off everything.
The dense pellet
that immured me

in tearless oblivion
exploded,
revealing irrevocably
sharp bits of anger
and jagged jealousy
embedded like old shrapnel.

Now grief has undone me.
I mourn not only your loss
but lost bits of mangled me.
I marvel at how a dead man
can still break my heart.

~

Love's Odd Logic

How many dinners did you ruin
harping on one inferior dish?
How often, amid pristine scenery,
did you besmear our minds
with criticisms of familiars?
How likely were you to dash cold water
on my enthusiasm for an invitation,
claiming you didn't want to go?

Why do I review your faux pas now?
Only to reveal the perennial hope,
like an unquenchable pilot light,
that love harbors at its heart—
for I never ceased to look forward
with keen expectation
to any meal or outing,
or just an evening at home,
as long as I was with you.

~

Dam

Formed by hard words from you,
mortared with my fears,
it stood firm, strangely,
lo these many years—
such a familiar fixture
I scarcely noticed it.

Until it all came tumbling down
dissolved by the deluge
of my tears.
The breaking torrent
bears fragments of us
dating back to courtship days:
endearments, imprecations—
kaleidoscopic debris
of all our years.

Now that you're gone
fresh feeling floods me
borne by a potent pulse.
The wonder is
I blocked off so long
the pressure of passion
pent in me.

～

On Looking at Our Wedding Photos

This marriage has reached completion,
coming to term but not perfection—
an entity marred beyond recognition
at crucial points by inattention.
Conceived in pure passion,
delivered up at last with devotion,
yet in gestation suffering distortion
like any other mortal creation.

~

Love's Refrain

"*Ti voglio bene*": "I want you well"—
one way Italians say "I love you"—
and the reply, "*Anch'io*": "Me too."
We repeated it daily,
a reminder that we were
in the right place at the right time.
I find myself saying it still,
nostalgic for reassurance.

I wonder if you can hear me
and need the comforting too.
Somehow I doubt it.
You rallied in emergencies.
If anyone could pull off
liberation at the eleventh hour
it would be you.
You're probably
getting on with your death,
whatever that involves,
and not looking back.
I have no idea where my words end up
but feel compelled to send them:
"*Ti voglio bene*," it seems, forever,
even if "*anch'io*"
never echoes.

~

Heart Attacks

They say each episode
kills some muscle.
I guess one carries death, then,
an inert burden at the core.
When the shock of your death
restarted my heart,
some chronic blocks
refused to budge:
fibers numbed by old slights ignored,
bits that died bit by bit,
buried but unmourned.

~

The Antidote

When I miss you too much
and the vocatives
verge on veneration—
"Dear soul," "Old-timer," "*Amore mio*"—
I am infected with desperation
and cast about for
any sort of medication.
I dose myself with recollection
of venomous things you said.
However, I have to admit
poison as an antidote
doesn't work very well.

~

Odd Couple

I miss the man in love with his cat,
who onomatopoeically said "cute";
the you who asked for my approval
when you cooked, importuning, "Taste!"
I listen for the teasing laugh
when caught in a minor faux pas,
seek in vain that look of relief
as I come through the front door late.
Mainly I lack your warm presence
by my side, in bed and at table.

I mourn the man who was right at all costs,
who sentenced my suggestions without trial,
so irate when I dared advise him
that he burnt a scar on his lip
to prove my warning invalid.
I still seem to hear a caustic remark
when I use my left for a right-hand job
and sense a cold sneer
when I put my foot in my mouth.

Why do I mourn Mr. Always Right?
Because, although so unlike you,
he disappeared in your company
and we never let him know
he was unworthy of you.

~

Solicitude

Each time I went out the door
on my way to work
you'd call after me,
"Drive carefully!"

It made life seem worthwhile
since you wanted so much for me to live
that you had a superstitious dread
of forgetting to warn me once
and perhaps that time I'd be dead.
Now my driving hasn't changed—
still defensively speedy—
but my mood is melancholy.
I weep at the wheel,
drenched in memory.
It's where I mourn you most:
you who gave the admonishing send-off,
who were glad to get my safe arrival call
and later that of imminent return.
You who worried if I came back late,
had the soup hot when I got home.
How it warmed my heart
to have you wait up
and know I was your all
as you were mine.

~

Your Soup

How can I describe
your soup?
It was nourishing,
it welcomed
and warmed me
when I came home late
and finally we sat down
to eat together.
It was substantial,
rich in lentils,
fresh carrots and celery:

in a word—perfect.
It reflected the love
with which you made it.
It stood for you.
I will miss it a lot,
that soup.

~

Old Soul

You were Jack *and* master of all trades
or rather you cornered their secrets,
cracked the conundrums
and were content.
You could play the piano,
sculpt, and print pictures.
Lawyers said you should have plied their trade.
You could figure out how anything was made
from pistons to puff pastry or platters.
Those who knew you best
guessed you'd been born often
and played many parts.
However, like Leonardo,
once you resolved a riddle,
performed the decisive test
or produced the prototype,
you moved on.

You seemed skittish to be confined
to one role or another;
so you shifted shapes
and spent this life
as a dilettante.

You wondered why you were here

with no urge to make a commitment.
Perhaps you had to play once more
your many motifs
and make a grand finale.

~

Sacrifice

At the Kauai Hindu Temple,
"Let me learn to love," I wrote—
meaning not infatuation, obsession,
or even sallies into affection,
but true fusion in compassion.
My supplication was burnt,
offered to the *devas*.

Months passed, you died,
and I forgot my petition.
I was busy weeping
because your unique being
will not manifest again
and you had to give up
the bright world in spring.

So, my obdurate heart has burst,
purification has at last begun.
My grief is graced with gratitude
although you are the price
I've paid for this bounty.

~

Chapter 4: Signs

Bird Tracks: A *Pantoum*

As my mother ended her ninetieth year
on my *bonsai* appeared a bold blue jay
who regarded me with no trace of fear.
I knew him, he'd been her protégé.

On my *bonsai* appeared a bold blue jay.
Contrary to kind, he made no squawk.
I knew him, he'd been her protégé.
He came as an augur—not to mock.

Contrary to kind, he made no squawk,
the first of prophets to come by wing.
He came as an augur—not to mock,
an envoy of flocks who do not sing—

the first of prophets to come by wing.
Then ravens alit on the giant pine,
two envoys of flocks who do not sing.
They were too clearly a fatal sign.

Then ravens alit on the giant pine
next door, where Fran my friend declined.
They were too clearly a fatal sign
for her and for one more yet to find.

Next door where Fran my friend declined
they conferred darkly on a limb
for her and for one more yet to find
and fling beyond the world's bright rim.

They conferred darkly on a limb.
It was you they chose to take away

and fling beyond the world's bright rim—
ravens, successors to the jay.

It was you they chose to take away.
They left me with this conundrum:
ravens, successors to the jay—
what rare bird was yet to come?

They left me with this conundrum.
I asked the rainbow-circled sun to say
what rare bird was yet to come?
A hawk on your cremation day!

I asked the rainbow-circled sun to say
the gist in the gyre of this braying raptor,
a hawk on your cremation day.
I welcomed him as your messenger.

The gist in the gyre of this braying raptor
remains a mystery not mine to pierce;
I welcomed him as your messenger.
Why he came when called, shrill and fierce

remains a mystery not mine to pierce.
Perhaps your totem Phoenix knows
why he came when called, shrill and fierce,
a bolt from where the hot sun glows.

Perhaps your totem Phoenix knows
you chose a card with its brazen guise,
a bolt from where the hot sun glows,
left words for your funeral to my surprise.

You chose a card with its brazen guise
to write a "reminder" to your self,
left words for your funeral to my surprise:

the *credo* that "flames can't destroy the Self."

To write a "reminder" to your self:
What prompted, years before your loss,
the *credo* that "flames can't destroy the Self"
but rather just "burn off our dross"?

∼

Auguries

There were plenty of signs:
the dying kitten in Rome,
the coffin lowered
into the alley at Levanto,
the yearned-for return
home to learn
your closest brother-friend
had met his end.
Then there were those
discarded cars on Kauai
half-covered in creepers.
And in your most life-like photo
you seem to eye nearby
portraits of the departed dear
as if setting a date
to join them.

We had warnings enough
to mend our ways.
Nevertheless, we carried on
undeterred in our habits.
Did we fail to fight,
accepting fate?
When ravens croaked in the tree
it was already too late.

~

Ganeshas

At the Kauai Hindu temple
we spied two stone statues
of the elephant-headed god,
one sitting four-square and solid
bedecked with leis and offerings,
the other beating a drum.
You bought a small brass Ganesha there,
and later got another in a shop,
dancing, foot lifted in a skip and a hop.

Did you pick this particular patron
through some intuition
of your declining condition—
Ganesha, Lord of Obstacles,
who both poses and
roots out opposition?

~

Dr. Sarafian

Then flew one of the seraphims unto me, having a live coal in his hand,
which he had taken . . . from off the altar. And he laid it upon my
mouth, and said, "Lo, this hath touched thy lips; and thine iniquity is
taken away, and thy sin purged." (Isaiah 6:6-7)

You were his favorite patient
and yet it was his lot
to say you would not survive.
He made no bones about the prognosis,
advised against life-prolonging ploys.
He dropped the bad news

like a hot coal
from the altar of God.
You were purged of triviality,
put your mind to bequeathing
and concern for me.
True to his name,
the doctor proved a messenger
of the highest order.
Coincidentally, it is said
the seraphim have multiple wings—
much like the practical Mentor
the famous psychic claimed
was your guardian.

~

Meditating Buddha Cat

I was surprised to find that little
crackle-glazed, jade-colored cat figure
on my engine hood in the public garage.
It was just the sort of thing
you'd have picked up in a thrift store
as totem for us cat-loving amateur yogis.
Perhaps, as my friend suggests,
you sent it from that great
Goodwill shop in the sky.
Just in case, I placed it on the mantel
seated in lotus position
by the unsigned cat card
you'd addressed to me.
It seems to say in its silent way
what you would have written:
Be calm, be well, seek high things
and don't forget your animal self.

~

Chapter 5: Dreams

True to Life

Early this morning
electric shivers thrilled my skin,
intimation of your imminent
ingress for the first time
into my dreams.
I went back to sleep
and there you were.
It seemed I made the mistake
of writing you off too soon.
Clearly you had survived
terminal illness.
I asked you the date
and you teased, "Nineteen-sixty-four."
True to life
we didn't pause
to embrace or rejoice.
We just tried to determine
whether we'd gone back in time
or if you had really
returned from the dead.

∼

Bedfellow

Clearly, you were real,
lying in bed by my side.
I could see the folds of your eye
as you recited an archaic poem
about someone "freaking" somewhere.
We cracked up over that one.
You were hearty and fleshy

so I knew I'd been deluded
to think you were dead.
Delighted to find you alive,
I pulled you into my arms
and hugged you to death.
You dissolved instantly
like mist in the wind.
I woke to disbelief,
chagrin the sharper
since I'd been so close
before the object
of my desires
was so rudely
snatched away.

~

Late-Breaking Lucid Dream

I was with you at dawn today again,
you so true-to-life
that I knew beyond doubt
you lived.
When it dawned on me
that you'd died,
I took you aside
for a serious talk.
As usual, you clowned around,
made out I was about
to make an alarming confession.
When I said, "Can you say
what happened in May?"
you let your tongue loll to the side
in cartoon spoof of one who's died—
and shocked me
to tremble awake.

When my heart settled down
I resumed the dream, in which
we carried on, unfazed by the fact
that the final curtain had crashed
on your comedy act.

~

Kissing Good-Bye

In this dream you were in your prime,
wearing light-gray pants and a jacket.
We were on our way to a party,
walking briskly.
When the sidewalk narrowed
I went ahead, but you called me
to stay by your side. You said,
"It's good I show my face."
I knew it was because
you'd gained the fame
of being dead.
I hugged and kissed you and
you responded warmly,
as in the old days.
We reached downtown
and you stepped inside a building.
Shortly it occurred to me
I would not see your face again.

~

Flying Supine

The dream was real from the start,
with the guest appearance in bed
of that beloved borrowed dog Tommy.
I could feel his thick fur, his affection

undiminished by the years.
You were there too
but then you withdrew
and I flew after,
lifting off like a template
from my body flat on its back
and rocketing through space like that,
all the while wailing in desperation:
"Take me to where you are!"
I could hear myself railing so loud
the neighbors would hear.
With that thought I awakened,
crestfallen, short
of my destination.

~

Negotiating

I thought the dreams had ended
but this fall morning you reappeared
in your green vest and red beret.
It seems you'd been to work
and were advising an employee
about benefits.

I was so happy to spot you
among the crowd
and to see you walk with vigor.
I knew they'd given you little to live
but now I was sure
that we'd share
another Christmas.

Then I recalled
that your body was ashes

in a box.

It seems I create such dreams
in an effort to bargain
for a few weeks
of grace.

~

In My Dreams

For a good while
you came
in youthful guise
bringing caresses
and importunity.
You were kind
to my parents,
told me
I was radiant.
We'd sit at table
and talk,
with no TV.

All that was rare
in our life
came thronging
into my dreams:
consolation prizes—
psyche patches.

~

Parole Denied

Determined to spring you
from death's dungeon,
"Ply mind over matter," I say,
"and you can heal yourself."
I offer to read the manual
but, typically, you reply,
"Let me read it myself;
if you do, I'll be bored to death."
At this point I awake to the fact
that death already closed its gate
and our plan for escape
was purely academic.
Undeterred, however,
I go back to sleep and
harangue you once more—
but realize on reasoning
there never had been
hope of acquittal.

~

Blind Dreams

You used to come so real
I touched your shape, your warmth.
Once I smelt coffee on your breath.
Your voice aroused my soul
with deep familiar timbre.
Twice I said, "But I'm asleep!"
You agreed: "We meet in dreams."
Finally I heard but failed
to locate you.

Now you have departed.
My dreams are opaque,

the nights of my life
lost to darkness.

~

Telegram

Last night you stayed for quite a while.
I was delighted to be a widow no longer,
sure that we'd done the right thing
to bring you home from the hospital.

Suddenly, out of the blue,
with customary sarcasm, you said,
"Do I have to send a telegram? "

Then I awoke, a widow once more,
curious to know the obvious fact
that, because of my denseness,
I had to decipher from a telegram.

~

Chapter 6: Ceremonies

As You Lay Dying

I stilled my tremors,
shoved tears back
into their sockets
lest you be distracted from
this all-important transition.
Nonetheless, each day
I reserved a restorative hour.
To you it seemed I "zoomed"
out of the hospital, eagerly.

On that Tuesday, to be your last,
I left in haste anyway,
hoping perhaps you'd slip off
while I was out.
As usual, in the five-deck garage
I couldn't find my car,
ended topside and there
under the sun, I came across
a fiftyish Black man washing a car.
I said, "Nice day to launder your vehicle."
"Oh," he replied, "it isn't mine;
just doing a colleague a favor."
We chatted, I spoke of you.
He took my two hands in his,
raised his face to the brilliant blue,
and prayed as if we were his own.
Then he drove me down the spirals
of that nightmare parking pile
in his gleaming Chrysler chariot
until I spotted our Corolla.
He offered his card, which declared
he was pastor in a local church.

At home I sat on our deck awhile,
contemplating the bright world
from which you would soon depart.
In fact, a half hour after my return,
you opened your eyes an instant
and passed away, as the saying goes.

Next day I unearthed the card
of that benevolent apparition
who had seized my hands
in a faltering moment
and prayed strength into me.
In fact I drove past his church,

just to be sure it stood foursquare
on this earthly plane.

~

Exhalation

You sleep, or so it seems,
but suddenly your eyes awake.
I come close but you
do not look at me.
With gaze raised
toward mid-brow,
lightly you inhale.
Your cheeks swell,
then with a sigh
you cast back
to the cosmos
this last breath
of borrowed air.

~

Posthumous Message

How farsighted of you to write
a reminder to yourself—
who knows how long ago—
that the Self survives the flames
that consume our gross matter,
and how fortuitous that I should find
that card with the Phoenix on it
in time to read the message
at your memorial.
I've propped up that image
with its widespread red wings
and egg-gripping talons

on top of the box
that holds your ashes.
Every once in a while I read it aloud
to remind myself as much as you
that dust is not
the essential You.

~

Taking Heart

Cleaning house, as you might guess
only because I expected guests,
I dusted the box that holds your dust.
My heart contracted,
my whole being diminished.
I felt compelled to read once more
the message you wrote to yourself
on the card with the Phoenix,
proclaiming the permanence of the Self.
I met the aqua gaze of the eyes
in the silver head you made,
which resembles you so much,
fire glowing from the opal in its brow—
your focus at point of death.

I replaced on the box
your card; the bust on a dry red rose,
symbol of your uniqueness;
and a shiny black Apache tear,
the roundness of wholeness.
After this
I was able to carry on
and put some heart
into dusting.

www.ingramcontent.com/pod-product-compliance
Lightning Source LLC
Chambersburg PA
CBHW060400090426
42734CB00011B/2199